Tales
of Beauty
&
Cruelty

Also by Kate Petty

Summer Cool
Summer Heat
Makeover

Tales of Beauty & Cruelty

KATE PETTY *and*
CAROLINE CASTLE

Orion
Children's Books

First published in Great Britain in 2005
by Orion Children's Books
a division of the Orion Publishing Group Ltd
Orion House
5 Upper St Martin's Lane
London WC2H 9EA

3 5 7 9 10 8 6 4 2

A catalogue record for this book is available
from the British Library

Printed in Great Britain by
Clays Ltd, St Ives plc

ISBN-10 1 84255 509 X
ISBN-13 978 1 84255 509 5

www.orionbooks.co.uk

In memory of my parents. KP
To Alison, with thanks! CC

Contents

Authors' Note

Love, hate, jealousy, greed, vanity, pity . . . these are the timeless themes that pervade the stories of Hans Christian Andersen, and which explain why they have endured for nearly two centuries.

As children, we both read and re-read the stories from old-fashioned hardbacks. Caroline's was illustrated with beautiful colour plates by Edmund Dulac; Kate's by Margaret Tarrant. We continued reading them well into our teens: 'The Little Match Girl', 'The Nightingale', 'The Snow Queen', 'The Emperor's New Clothes', 'The Little Mermaid', . . . whether humorous, forbidding or compassionate, they combined tales of the human condition with haunting imagery – shards of a broken mirror, drops of ruby-red blood, a flock of wild, changeling birds – and imagination, which is what makes them so timeless and compelling.

When discussing the bicentenary of Andersen's birth, we remembered how our teenage selves had remained enchanted by these age-old stories, how they still had the power to thrill us even though we had moved on to more adult reading. We wondered if the themes would translate to contemporary teenage life: love, hate, pity, jealousy, vanity – of course they would! So we set about finding our modern-day princes and princesses, our little match girls, our pompous emperors and our tragic mermaids. It wasn't difficult, as they walk among us just as they did over a hundred years ago. Our aim has been to bring them to life for a new generation, both as a tribute to the great storyteller, and because good stories can never be told too many times.

We hope you enjoy them.

Kate Petty and Caroline Castle
London, 2005

Swan

I'm so pretty, sometimes I take my own breath away. I know it sounds vain, but it's the truth, plain and simple. Mum thinks that any good-looking person who says they don't know it is lying. Spot on.

I find it difficult to pass a mirror without looking at myself. So when I'm around people I have to make a special effort; have to practically force myself not to look. And all the time I'm catching little accidental glimpses – there's this girl with the shining, gold hair (OK, highlights, but who's gonna know?), long neck and little upturned nose reflected in the window glass – and I think, wow! That's me! But there's something else that tells me I'm gorgeous. And it doesn't lie. It's the way people look at me. No mirror can compete with your own loveliness reflected back at you in people's eyes. Boys drool, men sort of melt and girls, well – they just look sick with jealousy.

So, I was standing in front of my bedroom mirror, looking at myself sideways, my head slightly tilted. I think I look my best in pale colours – sky blues, violets and pinks – sweet, but sexy. I was getting ready for a night out with the team: Rosa and May-Ann. We're all of us good-looking, but in different ways, which suits me fine. Rosa is tall and willowy with never-ending legs and long, brown, curly hair. She's flat-chested though, which drives her mad. I always act sympathetic when she goes off on one of her rants, but really I'm pleased. I hope she doesn't get a boob job. May-Ann is half Chinese, with beautiful honey-coloured skin and a curtain of silky black hair – she's the smallest, and really cute, but not really sexy, like me. We suit each other fine. When the three of us walk down the street together it's like a starburst.

So there I am, applying the finishing touches to my make-up when in she comes. The geek. And sits down on my bed in her stupid cut-off jeans that no self-respecting human being with an iota of style would wear.

'Get off my bed, Dork-Face! And get out of my room. Can't you see I'm getting ready?'

'Where're you going?'

'None of your business. Now push off.'

Here it comes . . .

'Can I come?'

'*Can I come! Can I come!*' I echo in her pathetic, whiny voice.

'You must be joking. Look at you! We don't want some kid hanging after us, cramping our style. Go do some homework or something.'

And then, like it's in the script, the watery eyes. The whinge. 'I am nearly *fourteen*, Katie – I wouldn't be a nuisance or anything.'

'You *are* a nuisance, Fat-Face. See, look at me – and look at you. You – fat little stumpy kid, me – well see for yourself.' I turned and gave her the pose, the hands on hips, full-on attitude. She crumbled. She slunk out with her tail between her legs like the pathetic bundle of spots and puppy fat that she is.

I turned back to the mirror. That was better – a clear, uncontaminated view.

Katie got the beauty and Rianna got the brains. I overheard my nan say this when I was ten. I knew it anyway, but it was good to have it confirmed. Beauty or brains – no contest. Give me beauty every time, although of course I wouldn't say I was *thick* by any means – I mean, if I wanted to I could do better at school . . . I just think, what's the point? I mean, why kill yourself studying a load of boring old stuff like . . . I dunno . . . like the destruction of the rainforest, or calculus, whatever that is.

That's why I couldn't care less when I came home yesterday and everyone was dancing around the kitchen as if we'd won the lottery or something. And Mum screeched, 'Oh, Katie! Katie! You'll never guess what! Rianna has won the Year Eight French prize. Our Rianna! A six-week study trip to France.'

Pathetic! Rianna was practically beside herself just

because of some geek prize that sounded as boring as hell. I mean, who in their right mind would want to spend their precious holidays on a *study* trip? Although, I must admit, I wouldn't mind going to France – to Paris, say – to check out those gorgeous clothes and have all those fit boys drooling over me.

Rianna, little show-off, was all fired up and alight. Like she had fireworks going off inside her. For a moment she looked almost pretty, although I knew it was just a trick of the light plus all the excitement giving her a momentary glow. I knew what to do with that.

'Great,' I said, smiling my smile that said: You may think you're great but really I could not care less and anything you do is absolutely pointless because in the end it just doesn't count. See, look at me. This is what counts. Long legs, tiny waist, big blue eyes, killer smile. Rianna was looking at me for something. Some kind of 'well done' thing, but I ignored her.

'That's nice,' I said to Mum. 'What's for tea?'

I flicked my hair back and glided over to the fridge, swaying my hips a little. I could feel Rianna shrinking behind me. And yes, when I turned, any hint of prettiness had gone. She was back to her pitiful, chubby, little ugly self.

So, Rosa, May-Ann and I were hanging out in Wicked – checking out the talent – or they were checking us out. Every few seconds, someone would look our way, or would walk past and do a double-take. It was only a matter of time before they started coming over – making jokes – trying to join in. We liked to play it cool, act as if we couldn't care less, although the reason we were there was leaning against the bar, deep in conversation with a girl in a blue micro-skirt and a black top cut oh-so-low. Cheap. But Rosa swore, with a hissed 'Don't look now but . . .' that he was checking us out every time he got the chance.

Sean Black. Even his name was cool. He'd suddenly appeared from nowhere a couple of weeks ago. Tall, dark-brown hair, dark eyes – almost black. Slim hips that looked fantastic in jeans. He hung around with some of the guys from the college and we figured he'd moved here to start a course in September although we didn't know for sure and were too cool to ask. We were just planning our next move when May-Ann hissed, 'Quick, geek alert!'

Oh no. Rianna in her stupid cut-offs suddenly loomed into view across the street. Then – horror. She stopped and squinted at the window.

'Quick, hide!' I almost yelled, ducking under the table as if I was looking for something. I was thinking, she wouldn't *dare* come over, would she? She knew me and my friends were out of bounds to her at all times – she knew the rules.

'I can't believe it!' hissed Rosa. 'She's coming over!'

'She's not! She's *not,* is she?' I was frantic. I had seen Sean shoot a sharp little look my way. I was convinced he'd clocked me and was interested – I mean, how could he not be? All I needed now was some fat little fashion-challenged nerd claiming me for a sister and it would blow everything.

'She's crossing the street,' May-Ann groaned in disbelief. 'And she's wearing sandals – with socks!' This was the end. I stayed hunched up under the table. I prayed silently to myself: 'Go away. Go away. Go away.'

Too late. God wasn't at home, or else he had some warped sense of humour, because I heard the door swing open and the ominous sound of sandals squeaking across the floor. It couldn't have been worse.

'Katie?'

I had no choice but to sit up, and anyway my back was killing me.

I looked daggers at her. Perhaps there was a chance that the force of my stare would somehow make her disintegrate. But no. She just stood there, large as life.

'You forgot your mobile,' she said, taking it out of her pocket. 'Mum sent me after you. You're to phone her and let her know what you're doing.'

This was *unbelievable*. How *could* she! I was cringing all over. Little pinpricks of embarrassment were shooting up and down my arms. Not only did it look as if I had Princess Nerd for a sister, but my *mum* was on my case. God! I glanced quickly at the bar. He was looking at us! My God.

I snatched the mobile. For a moment she looked as if she was going to sit down. This was beyond anything. 'Push off!' I snarled.

'I was only being helpful. At least you could say thanks,' she said, not budging.

Rosa looked as if she might explode. 'Get away from us!' she hissed. 'Can't you see you're embarrassing us?'

For a moment, Rianna looked as if she was going to cry. Then she looked sort of crestfallen. But she still didn't budge. All the time I was watching the bar. Drastic action was needed.

'For God's sake. Look at you! We're having a private conversation. We don't want some kid looking like rubbish hanging around us. *Shove off – now*, and I mean it!'

A fat tear appeared in the corner of her eye. She was

about to blub. Good. She'd finally got the message. She shot us a pathetic look and turned to go. '*I was only doing you a favour,*' she whimpered.

'Well, you've done it. Thanks. Now bog off, if you don't mind.'

And that was it. I watched her shuffle down the road with her head down. I looked up at the bar again. The tarty girl had disappeared and Sean was now talking to a really tall, skinny boy in a leather jacket. I felt him look at me just before I turned away. Who knows what damage had been done? On the other hand, beauty conquers all – as they say.

I flicked my hair back. It was looking particularly good that day. We all huddled around for a bitch about what a pathetic little pain Rianna was, and how she was going to get it when I got home and all the usual stuff and then May-Ann suddenly looked up and screeched. 'I don't *believe it*! He's gone! He's gone!' This was the pits. Our plan had been to make a night of it, like a military campaign. To follow him on to the next scene and on again if necessary. But he'd slipped away without us even noticing. God knows where he was now. Little cow. She'd managed to screw up my evening twice over.

Next day I caught her as she was coming out of the bathroom. I pushed her back in and held her against the wall. 'Don't you ever do that again, you stupid little *cow*. How many times do I have to tell you to get it into your *thick head*? Stay away from me and my friends. OK? We don't want you near us. No one wants you! Geddit?'

'But Mum . . .'

'*But Mum . . .*' I mimicked. 'But Mum nothing – you didn't have to *come in*, did you? In those stupid clothes, my

God, I thought I'd die! You could have called me outside, couldn't you? You're just trying to mess up my life, on purpose! You want everyone to know I've got a stupid, fat, little geek-brain sister hanging on to my every move. It's a good job you're off to France or God knows what'd happen.'

Tears, tears. Well, good. At least that meant the message had hit home.

Monday, she went to France. Mum and Dad wanted me to go to the airport with them to see her off. 'Come on, Katie, surely you want to say goodbye to your sister?'

I could have laughed myself silly. Why should I want to see any more of her than was absolutely, unavoidably necessary? As soon as she was out of the house wasn't soon enough for me. But parents, they don't get it. You have to play the game.

'Sorry!' I called down the stairs. 'I want to, but I've, I've . . . I've – uh – promised to help May-Ann with some homework . . .' You'd think she was going off on a lone expedition to the South Pole, the way they were fussing over her. God, they never fuss over me like that. 'Have you got your sun cream, you must be really careful, you know? Don't forget to phone, every day to let us know you're all right. Now have you got your passport – you're sure . . .?'

I watched from the top of the stairs. She stood there like butter wouldn't melt in her mouth. She'd pulled her hair into a ponytail, with two little hair slides. Trying to make herself look cute. She looked up at me. 'Bye, Katie!'

'Bye, Rianna!' I called sweetly. 'Have a good time.'

I came down and waved the car off from the doorway. I hope you just drop dead, was my last thought.

*

That evening the gang met up at Rosa's house. We raided the fridge and found a couple of pizzas and some Coke which we polished off to celebrate Rianna's departure and the start of our full-on Sean campaign. Then we set off in search of our prey. Rosa was wearing this red Lycra micro-skirt which made her legs look as if they went up to her armpits and then some. It was a bit much, I thought, although I would never say. The worse she looked the better, as far as I was concerned. Just made me look more cool, in a sexy, understated way.

We started off at Wicked. May-Ann squinted at the window. 'He's there! *He's in there!*' she screeched. God! Sometimes I think I'm growing out of these two. I mean, really, there's cool and there're screeching baby teens who practically faint at the sight of a half-decent male creature. But I had to admit, Sean wasn't just anyone. There he was, hanging out at the bar with the gang from college. He looked gorgeous; dark and broody, in a black T-shirt and a pair of Ikos. My heart actually missed a beat.

'Calm down,' I hissed. 'Be cool.' I grabbed Rosa's arms and the three of us swept in and glided past the crew at the bar to our usual spot by the window. A few heads turned, I can tell you; and some of the guys – well – their mouths practically hit the floor when Rosa sat down and crossed her long legs.

'It's almost as if he is *deliberately* ignoring us,' Rosa said, furious when her little ploy didn't even get a sideways glance from the adored one. I pretended to commiserate but really, I knew why. I knew he wouldn't be interested in that sort of cheap move. He was deep. A cut above.

And when it was my turn to get the drinks in, I pushed my way through the crowd and sidled up next to him. I actually felt faint. A few of the lads in his crowd smiled and made comments, the usual thing: 'All right darlin',' 'Hi, gorgeous.' I was glad the other guys were noticing me. Nothing unusual in that, of course, but I was thinking that Sean was bound to turn to see who was causing all the fuss. But all he did was move closer to the guy he was talking to, to give me some room. Really! Something was wrong. As soon as I'd dispensed the drinks I rushed to the loo to check myself over.

But there was nothing. Nothing to worry about. I was looking *so* good. I hadn't suddenly sprouted an acre of spots, or put on weight, and I wasn't having a bad hair day. I *never* have a bad hair day. But there was something eating away at me. An uncomfortable, sick feeling, like there was some awful thing waiting. Like the feeling you have when you wake up the morning after something dreadful has happened, and for a split second you can't remember what it is. And then for some reason I started thinking about Rianna. It was too weird.

By the end of the evening we'd fended off at least five approaches from various lads, operating in ones and twos. We were saving ourselves for the big one. And, yep, as the bell went for closing, the whole crowd from the bar drifted over. 'Hey, girls! Wanna come on to Stones with us? We've got a taxi booked.' They were laughing and teasing and Rosa nearly fell over herself with her hair-flicking and leg-crossing, eyes darting all over the place trying to make contact with our prey. But Sean? He stayed in the background, hanging back, like *on purpose*. I started singing silently inside my head, look at me, look at me. Can't you *see*?

One of the lads sat on the edge of my seat and started stroking my hair. 'What's your name, gorgeous?' I suddenly realised it was Dylan Pryne, a boy I had had a sort of crush on when I was twelve; but now he seemed gawky and baby-faced. I suppose at a push he was OK and maybe, in another time, I would have gone for it – but not now. Not now that Sean was around.

But when I turned, Sean had disappeared! Gone, just *dissolved,* like mist. One minute he was there, on the edge, and the next he was gone. I got that sick feeling again. Almost as if someone had died.

We did go to Stones with them, all of us hoping that maybe Sean'd gone on ahead, made his own way. The place was half empty, and we saw at once, our eyes scanning the floor, razor sharp, that he wasn't there. We danced with a few of the guys, but I couldn't get rid of that tight feeling in my stomach. Then we sat huddled over the table, uselessly watching the door, just in case . . . Half an hour later we were all silently, individually, admitting defeat. Our spirits began sinking, and then plunged to rock bottom.

We left by ourselves.

Sunday, I slept late – very late. Even when I woke I lay in bed for a long, long time thinking and thinking – about Sean, about what I was doing wrong. All the time that funny, uncomfortable feeling kept creeping in like I had some invisible sword of doom hanging over me. Eventually, I managed to drag myself to the bathroom. I examined myself from every angle. Even when I was feeling wrecked,

I still looked OK – pale and rather tragic-looking, but sweet. As I was getting into the shower, Rianna's collection of rubber ducks stared at me with their stupid cartoon eyes. There was her heart-shaped sponge and her pathetic Princess Pansy bubble bath. God! Even when she wasn't here, just the thought of her made me mad. Miss Clever-Clogs-Butter-Wouldn't-Melt-In-My-Mouth-Goody-Two-Shoes Rianna. I ran the shower over one of the ducks until it tumbled into the bath. Then I dug my heel into it; slowly, heavily. It squeaked in protest but I kept going, bit by bit, and then it gave one last long, trumpeting squeak and was dead; flat as a pancake; its stupid head sticking up as if to say, 'Waddaya do that for?' and I was saying to myself: Because I can. I can do things. Finished. I felt better immediately. My mood began to lift. It was as if I had been on holiday from myself and was now back. Back inside my body.

I took Rianna's blue silk dressing-gown from the back of the door and wrapped it around me. It always annoyed me that she had that robe – it was a present from Nan, and far too good for her, as far as I was concerned. I went back to bed and thought about Sean for about two hours. Me and him. What a cool couple we would make. I imagined the whole thing. Like the moment he would suddenly clock on to me, and ask me out. How Rosa and May-Ann would have to pretend to be pleased but are eaten up with jealousy, as they have to listen to all the fantastic details. How the two of us would walk into Stones and every head would turn. How he would look at me, in that deep way of true love, right in the eyes, like he was seeing his soul mate. The look.

Then, of course, Mum screams up the stairs about what on earth am I doing and it's half-past two in the afternoon and it's about time I got up and made myself useful. Spell broken.

We spent the rest of the summer Sean-hunting. We couldn't help ourselves. You could say that the less interested he seemed, the more obsessed we became. I had my highlights redone the minute a millimetre of root started to show. I had manicures, facials; my whole body was beautiful, brown and silky smooth with fake tan. If he was going to go for one of us, I was making sure it would be me.

But we got nowhere. The odd scrap occasionally thrown our way – a half-smile, a slight nod of acknowledgement, then nothing – no follow-through. May-Ann thought perhaps he was just playing it cool to get our interest. But this was *too* cool. Below freezing point. Then there was the 'gay' theory. Rosa insisted there could be no other explanation. 'I mean, just look at us!' she said. But then we heard that he had split up from his long-term girlfriend just before he moved here for college. Someone actually *knew* her. And we discussed endlessly how he should be over it by now – now he had such an irresistible attraction as the A-Team on his case.

And then it was nearly the end of the holidays. It crept into our blue-sky days like distant thunder. Mum said I should start thinking about school, but I was on another planet. School! We'd been living in a different dimension. We were grown-ups, strutting our stuff out in the world. We knew without saying anything that all three of us had already left. Gone to another place. The idea of uniforms and teachers pushing us around, telling us what to do, seemed a stupid joke. And A-levels? I couldn't care less. I knew somehow I had big things ahead of me, and they had nothing to do with sitting up all night worrying about grades.

And then Mum announced that Rianna would be coming back on Saturday. It was funny, I'd had this feeling that something annoying was about to happen.

We had the airport thing again. Like I'd be desperate to spend the last shreds of the holiday hanging around the arrivals gate waiting for the first glimpse of fat little Geek-Face shining with the wondrous happenings of her stupid trip. And anyway, the Team was all geared up for a wild end-of-holiday night and I had my new red, backless silk dress that I'd spent practically all my savings on hanging up behind the door, ready. For I'd decided tonight was the night. Tonight, I was going to go for it with Sean and I was going to look so drop-dead, so off-the-scale that he wouldn't be able to resist. So I said how awful that I had forgotten, how I'd really *love* to go but I'd arranged to meet the gang in town for a special 'back to school' thing and it was too late to change now.

And Mum said, 'Well, all right, but be sure you spend some time with her tomorrow. Maybe we can all go out to lunch. I'm sure she's missed you.' Then she went on about how Rianna's 'made a little friend' – some other prize-winning geek girl from her school who had ended up in the same town, and how nice it was she'd have someone to travel with, and I was thinking, good for her. I absolutely could not care less.

So there I was, with the Team. The A-Team. Sitting in our booth at the club, feeling all fizzed up and alive with excitement at my plan. I had my eyes on him. That was for sure. I felt gorgeous; I knew I was attracting a lot of attention in my little red number. I kept my back nice and straight, and every now and then turned my head sideways with a slight toss of the hair, which I knew was a cute, charming little ploy. And I began to believe it was working! I took a risk and shot a cheeky look his way. He just happened to be turning round at that precise point, and he caught it and – yay! – gave me a half-smile back. Another minute or two and I'd be over there. I was full of it that night.

Then suddenly, there was this funny silence. A split second of quiet, like the only thing alive was the air and everything else was frozen. And I saw a few heads turn towards the door, including Sean's. And there were these two girls standing there, tanned, shiny girls with long legs. Something made me look back at Sean. He had *the look*, the look I'd been waiting for all summer.

In that eerie second the two strange, new girls seemed surrounded by light. I looked back at the bar. Sean was staring straight at the taller girl with the brown hair. She had this glow, like someone had turned a light on inside her. Then my body felt weird, like a sudden sickness was seeping into my limbs. One of them was short and fair, sweet-looking.

The other one was Rianna.

I'm a pretty girl, but Rianna is beautiful. I had seen it coming – in her eyes, in the way her hair fell from the crown of her head; in the curve of her lip – the light behind her skin. I'd been watching, studying every tiny little detail of her growing. And my terrible fear of it made me cruel, and it was like an illness, and I thought somehow I could stop it. But that was stupid; nothing can stop beauty.

I'm a pretty girl, but Rianna is beautiful. It's a tragedy really; and something I'll have to live with all of my life.

This story was inspired by 'The Ugly Duckling'. CC

The Real Thing

When his mother sang at the top of her voice in the kitchen, Max shut his bedroom door firmly. It was embarrassing to hear her warbling so shamelessly as she filled the house with canteen smells: curried lasagne; toad-in-the-hole; rhubarb fluff and all the other disgusting dinners in her school-cook repertoire. If she bellowed along to music in the car, he would remove his state-of-the-art headphones for just long enough to plead, 'Shut up, Mum. I hate it when you sing.' Then he would wince as if in pain and turn up the volume on his iPod.

Max's bedroom was his refuge and his studio. It contained everything he needed to mix the sounds he loved: decks, computer, mixer. *Big* amplifier. And his only concession to live sounds – his drum kit.

Today had been a pig of a day. A cold wind and a lashing rain had followed him all the way to school and whipped in his face all the way home. Max pounded on his drums to drown out the sound of the gale still roaring round the house and the rain pelting against the window. Bam. Bam. Ratatap. Paradiddle. Paradiddle diddle. He was trying to drown out the memory of Jenny Moon's voice, too, when they'd been forced to carry chairs for tomorrow's concert across the playground together. Overweight Jenny Moon from his music class, rain on her glasses, wisps of brown hair blowing across her face. 'Ma-ax,' she'd panted, 'how come I'm carrying four chairs and you're only carrying one?'

'Because you're stupid and I'm not.'

'Max, wait for me,' she'd wailed, wobbling after him. He'd let the door swing in her face. That had shown her.

Max despised Jenny Moon. How could her so-called 'music' – her singing – come under the same heading as his complex mixes? All Jenny had to do was open her mouth; his work took hour after painstaking hour, sampling and cutting at the computer.

There was a knock on his door and it was his dad, home from his dry-cleaning empire: seven shops. Max's dad knew his son was a genius. He liked spending money on all that techno gear, wished he'd had that kind of opportunity. 'Suppertime, my son,' he said. 'You need brain food to operate that lot. Respect, boy. Don't know how you do it.'

Max went downstairs and sat at the table with his two older sisters, Hazel and Julie. His mother brought in the steak-and-kidney pie with Brussels sprouts and mash. Max's father ate it with relish. Hazel and Julie and Max barely touched it. The smell of the food had already settled on their hair and their clothes, and that was quite enough. All three were lean.

A few roads away at St Andrew's Vicarage – an ugly house with fishtail tiling and picture windows – Jenny Moon doled out spaghetti to her dad and her younger brother Joshua. Thirteen-year-old Joshua had the body of a man-mountain and the brain of a toddler. Jenny loved Joshua, but he tried her patience to the limit. He made life less arid, but no easier. Joshua put his hand in the tomato sauce and smeared it over his face. Jenny and her dad tucked into the comforting food, letting Joshua get on with it. There would be storms and tantrums soon enough. Their mother, the Reverend Hilary Moon, was taking evensong over the way.

Jenny Moon's dad fondly called his daughter 'Dumpling', which said it all, really. Her grey school uniform made her look plumper than she really was. She wore her brown hair pulled back into a ponytail and her shining brown eyes were dulled and slightly magnified behind her glasses.

When she was younger, her dad had called her 'my little Jenny wren', and that had suited her then, too, when she'd been small and round with brown glossy hair and bright beady eyes, and the piping voice of a wren in spring. The teenage Jenny was not so sprightly as the little girl she'd been. Feeling fat and wearing a grey uniform all day long made her lacklustre. But she still had the voice. Years of singing solos with the church choir had distilled her liquid treble into pure gold. Jenny Moon could sing like a dream. Everyone who heard her forgot the world around them while she held them in thrall. And when her song was over, it hung in the air and wiped out the memory of all the others.

Jenny herself had a prodigious musical memory. She could remember every carol, every song, every oratorio, every recitative she had ever learnt. She could score it too, if you asked her, pencil flying over the staves as she scratched in the notes for all the parts. Jenny's compositions were simple, but she was truly a musician. Tonight, as she ate her pasta, she tuned in to the notes and cadences of the rain and wind outside the plate-glass window. She listened to their song in order to drown out the gross, lip-smacking, slurping noises of Joshua as he crammed pasta and tomato sauce into his mouth.

The concert was a chance for the exam candidates to perform their work in front of an audience. Later on they would record it and send it off to be marked. For the first time, parents would understand what their offspring had been working on. It would be a long evening, as twenty-seven students performed their pieces. Some were simple songs or music for a single instrument, others were scored for a whole orchestra or brass band or jazz ensemble. And then there was Max, where the only 'instrument' on show was a pair of amplifiers.

'Brilliant!' said Max's dad afterwards as he threw his keys on the hall table. 'Brilliant, son. I only wish I'd had your chances. All you kids.'

'It was lovely, dear,' said his mum, 'especially that little singer. Like Charlotte Church, she was. Lovely song. Did she really write it all herself?'

'Where have you been, Mum? We all wrote our own stuff. That's what the concert was about.'

'No one as clever as you, son,' said his dad. 'People would be queuing to buy yours in HMV any day.'

'No need, Dad, they download it off the Internet already.' It was true. Max had his fans out there. 'Let's see your video, then.'

'Uh?' Max's dad looked guilty.

'You did video the concert, didn't you?'

'Well, son, sort of. I mean, I decided not to bother because – well, you weren't exactly performing, were you?'

'Hello-o? I was sitting there, Dad. And my music was coming out the amps.'

Max's dad curled his hand around the little video camera in his coat pocket.

'And what do you mean by "sort of"? You did video some of it, didn't you?' asked Max, guessing already who it would be.

'No one much, son. Well, we can hear you any time, but your mother wanted me to get the singing girl.'

Max looked threatening. His parents were both a little afraid of him. 'Show us.' And there on the tiny screen was Jenny Moon perched on a stool with her guitar, glasses glinting in the spotlights, her voice tinny and diminished inside the masterpiece of micro-technology.

No one seemed to get it, as far as Max was concerned. No one seemed to understand the sheer perfection of music without instruments, without people. He could produce any sound he wanted. True, it sometimes came from humans in the first place, but he was totally in control. Max could sample a piece, reassign every note to a key on his keyboard and play them into a different tune altogether. The power of it was awesome. He, Max, could make Ray Charles or John Lennon sing different songs, *his* songs. He could twist them, turn them, invert them, play over them. It was so cool, so inventive. Not even the music teacher seemed to really understand, even though Max showed her on screen, showed her the computer notation in its sections, how he could cut it up, squeeze it, add his own rhythms. She kept saying, perhaps you should work with some of the sounds in this class, the other kids, interact a bit. She just didn't get it.

But that was how Max ended up in a practice room with Jenny Moon and a microphone and a computer.

'I didn't ask to do this,' he told her right off.

'Me neither,' she retorted, stung.

'Well, sing something, then.'

'What – *any*thing?'

'Yeah,' he said, his eyes averted from Jenny as he fiddled with the switches. He didn't like looking at her. 'It's only your voice I'll be using. Just sing up and down if you want.'

'You mean sing a *scale*?' said Jenny scathingly to his back. 'In an *octave*, or two, perhaps?'

'Whatever,' said Max, still not looking at her.

'You don't even know, do you?' said Jenny. 'You don't even know what a scale is, or an octave. Or a crotchet or a quaver, or a phrase or a cadence. Probably wouldn't know middle C if it bit you on the bum. But you'll still end up with an A-star for music.'

'Yeah, yeah,' said Max. 'When you've quite finished.'

Jenny felt a little foolish. Max handed her the mike. Jenny sang the music she'd written into it. It was a setting of a verse from Keats:

> '*Thou wast not born for death, immortal Bird!*
> *No hungry generations tread thee down;*
> *The voice I hear this passing night was heard*
> *In ancient days by emperor and clown:*
> *Perhaps the self-same song that found a path*
> *Through the sad heart of Ruth when sick for home*
> *She stood in tears amid the alien corn;*
> *The same that ofttimes hath*
> *Charm'd magic casements, opening on the foam*
> *Of perilous seas, in faery lands forlorn.*'

Max switched off the record button. 'Bible stuff, I suppose,' he said dismissively, his work done.

'No, as it happens,' said Jenny. 'Just because my mum's a vicar doesn't mean I sing hymns all the time.'

'Ha ha!' Max hooted. 'Your mum's a vicar! Ha ha! That would explain it then. Why you're such a smug cow. Life all rosy and cosy down at the vicarage then?'

Tears sprang to Jenny's eyes. She didn't know what she'd done to deserve this. She looked up, looked levelly at Max, looked him in the eye to see if she could find the answer there.

'What?' he said.

'Why? Why are you being cruel to me?'

'"Cru-el to me,"' he mimicked. 'Well, you despise me, don't you? Everybody loves Jenny Moon's singing. Voice like an angel. Blahblahdeblah. You don't think it's music, what I do, do you? Well, you can stuff what you think up your fat bum. You in your nice vicarage. You should eat less, you know. Stay away from the pies.'

Jenny had been going to protest that actually she liked Max's stuff, she thought it was really inventive, didn't know how he did it, but the words died in her throat.

Max wound up the leads and headed towards the door. 'And if you weren't so fat you might not smell so bad,' was his parting, childish shot. The burst of noise as the door opened on to the corridor was like shellfire – it swallowed him up. He left the door swinging and Jenny heard the rise and fall of footsteps and voices calling and let the sound swirl around her, soothing, before leaving the room, leaving the school and facing an evening at home of Joshua's mess and tantrums. She felt as if Max had assaulted her, stolen her voice.

Max had captured Jenny's voice. He had it trapped on CD. He was careful not to play it when his mum was around – she'd want to listen. Max dispersed Jenny's sung notes onto his keyboard. Now if he played one note it would come out as '*death*' and another as '*mort*', yet another as '*Bird*'. He could play the tune of 'Three Blind Mice' and it came out as '*death mort Bird*' – so clever. He could play a burst of notes, a fusillade of chords in which all Jenny's words came out at once – fantastic. He found himself strangely mesmerised by her disembodied voice when it was detached from her earthbound, visceral self. The high note of *'charm'd'* rang in his ears. He cut it into his own music so that it chimed like a bell. Who needed the real Jenny Moon now?

'Hope you're backing that all up, son,' said his dad over a supper of baked-bean pizza followed by lime jelly and cream.

'Yeah, yeah,' said Max. Of course he had everything on CD. All those sounds digitised onto plastic. Fantastic plastic. Max had a sneaking fondness for lime jelly and cream. He did a little drumroll with two spoons before scraping back his chair and heading upstairs to his music.

Jenny wasn't sure how she felt when she heard Max's final version of his exam piece, the way her voice singing *'charm'd'* chimed like a bell. He'd made little rhythmical arrangements with the words *'death'* and *'Bird'*, too – a staccato burst of *'deaths'* – *'dea-dea-dea-death'* and a trilling *'Bird'* like a mobile phone. She listened closely, working out how Max had put it all together. It was totally brilliant, so much more inventive than anyone else's – no wonder Max was arrogant. She knew, though, that her voice had got to him. He must have listened to it so many times, which was a small triumph for her. Max looked in her direction from under hooded eyelids. He felt a little differently about Jenny Moon these days – less disgust, a kind of interest – but he didn't want her knowing that.

Their music teacher reminded them about the deadline for exam entries straight after half-term – tapes, CDs, scores, whatever – but she needed them in on the first day back.

Max's dad had bought a brand-new caravan to attach to this

year's SUV. He persuaded the whole family to spend half-term in Devon, even though Hazel and Julie insisted on staying in a hotel. It was a while since they had all been on holiday together. Max's mum could still cook, but Max would have to take a break from his computer screen for a while, maybe get out into the fresh air.

Jenny had no such luck. She was stuck at home as usual with her mother's ceaseless work for the church, her dad's house-husbandry and her brother Joshua. She worked on her song but it seemed childish and simple compared with Max's. She found herself playing his piece in her head more often than Max deserved. She made herself take a walk every day – anything to get out of the house, and she could do with the exercise – and it took her past Max's house. It looked shut up, as if the owners were away, so she felt less self-conscious than she might have done. She was strangely curious about the place where her disembodied voice was held – a new, fussy sort of house, so different from her own.

That night, at Max's house, security lights came on and burglar alarms shrieked, but by the time the police-car sirens had wailed their way over in response, all Max's computer gear and CD collection had been stolen. All of it. The thieves were long gone. Max's dad received a phone call from the police, but he really wasn't too worried: he knew he was well insured. Max could get an upgrade, and he downloaded most of his music these days; who needed CDs? Since Max had immediately got in with the only club in this seaside resort – and was helping out with the DJ-ing into the small hours and sleeping most of the day – it wasn't worth worrying him.

Max's dad told him about the burglary on the way home, making light of it. 'Not much taken. All dealt with. Police were marvellous.' So Max's dismay when he returned to his devastated bedroom was considerable. 'Don't worry, son,' said his dad. 'Have to get used to being burgled once in a while when you live in a house like this. Just think what we'll get on the insurance. You ought to be happy – it's the perfect excuse to upgrade all your gear.'

'Da-ad – the stuff for my music exam!'

'But you said you backed it all up?'

'On CD, Dad. They've nicked every single one of my CDs. All my vinyl, too. Everything.' Max could have cried, if he'd been that sort of boy. How could he ever recreate that whole piece, the chimes of Jenny's '*charm'd*', the gunfire of her '*death*', the ringtone of her '*Bird*'? Max had to get out.

Max swung out of his gate and straight into Jenny on her daily walk. 'Come to gloat, have you?' he asked her, noticing that she looked a little more normal out of school uniform, in jeans instead of a bunched-up grey skirt, her hair loose and shiny. Jenny regarded him with incomprehension. Max barged past her. 'Well, even if you aren't gloating now, you will be, soon enough.'

Max walked and walked, an activity that was quite unusual for him. The enormity of what he had lost kept on coming at him, and with it the realisation of how little his father understood of what he did and cared about. He could retrieve the music that was on the Internet by accessing it himself. That was the easy part. No, it was his sources, his CDs, all the unfinished material and ideas that he had saved. And it was his exam piece – the closest to perfection he had ever come. If only his father had videoed it at the concert, even without the latest additions. But no, he had to go and record Jenny Moon. Max reached the woods that fringed the fields on the edge of town. He sat down on a bench in the twilight and wept, little staccato bursts of sobbing as the wind got up in the trees and rattled the branches around him.

It was the Reverend Hilary Moon who first got wind of the burglary at Max's house and the implications for Max and his exam. Some of her congregation had been discussing it after evensong. She came home more quickly than usual, while Jenny and her dad and Joshua were eating ice cream, Joshua for once content and quiet.

'Your friend Max has been burgled,' she said.

'My *friend*?' asked Jenny, with a hollow laugh.

'The clever boy in your music class, the one with the computer.'

Jenny found herself feeling anxious on Max's behalf. 'His computer wasn't stolen, was it?'

'That's what I heard. And a massive CD collection, too. I don't know – it's not right that some children should have so much . . . *stuff*.'

'But that's his music, Mum. It's like someone having their Stradivarius stolen. And what will he do about his exam piece? It was all on there.'

'I'm sure if it was any good, he'll remember it. Won't they have recorded it at school?'

'There was no need. He only had to put it on CD. And he'll never remember it. It was too complicated.'

'Do you mean he didn't bother to write it down?'

Jenny felt exasperated. 'He didn't *need* to, Mum. Don't you get it?'

'Not much sympathy from this quarter then,' said the Reverend Hilary Moon, squeezing out a J-cloth in preparation for wiping Joshua's sticky chin and hands and T-shirt.

'I'm going out,' said Jenny. 'Don't worry, I've got my phone.'

Jenny walked through the windy night. She heard the song of the wind as it billowed and swelled and whistled down the telegraph wires. The restored security light blazed on her head as the doorbell chimed inside Max's house. His sister Julie opened the door and a custard-scented cloud wafted out to where Jenny stood. 'I've come to help Max,' she said.

'I think Max is beyond help,' said his sister. 'He's inconsolable. I've never seen him like this before, and my parents are acting like he's died. But you can go up. His room is the second on the left.'

Jenny knocked on the door. Inside she could hear a mournful tapping as Max beat on his desk with a pencil. She opened the door. Max looked terrible.

'I can help you,' said Jenny.

'*You*?' said Max, ungracious to the last. 'How?'

'I can remember your piece pretty well. I can write it down. I can score it for the piano, and then you can record it and work from that.'

'You can remember what I wrote – in your *head*?' Max was incredulous.

'Yes,' said Jenny simply. 'I can't make it up like you can, but I can remember it. I've sung big music all my life – Christmas Oratorio, B minor Mass. I'll need a bit of help from you, obviously, but I can remember it. It's something I can do.'

Max was silenced by respect. 'You'd do that? For me?'

Jenny spent Sunday at the piano with a pad of music paper. She didn't go to church. When Joshua bothered her she directed him towards the ice cream. Max came round before lunch. Jenny dug out a toy drum for him to beat his complex rhythms on and Max had the full benefit of a Joshua tantrum when he spotted it before Jenny sent him off with more ice cream. Max and Jenny had ice cream for lunch themselves. With chips.

Together they recreated his rhythms and scratches and repeats on paper in a form that Jenny could play on the piano keyboard well enough for him to record as soon as he was able to lay his hands on some kit again and salvage his exam piece. Max no longer saw a fat girl with glasses. He saw a kind of angel.

Again he asked her why; why she'd do this for someone who'd been as mean to her as he had. Jenny thought hard about her answer. She didn't want Max thinking she'd fallen in love with him, or anything stupid like that. And anyway, she hadn't. 'It's because,' she said slowly, 'we have a lot in common that is really important, far more important than our differences. And because we're both lucky enough to be able to touch people's hearts and free them for a while from all the horrible stuff that goes on around them.' She smiled. It was good to have Max listening to her for a change. 'But I suppose it was mostly because I respect what you do and I wanted you to respect me.'

'Will you sing for me again?' said Max.

'And that, too,' said Jenny. 'I knew that despite everything, my singing – what I do best – had got to you, which is all any of us wants, really, isn't it?'

This story was inspired by 'The Nightingale'. KP

Coming Up for Air

'Are you OK?'

I looked up, into the face of an angel. That's the only way to describe him. He still had his hand around my arm where he had stopped me from falling. I was falling now, in a different way, looking into that face that said nothing but 'Are you OK?' No disgust, no judgement, just a feeling that was real and true that made him ask, 'Are you OK?' and mean it.

My name is Jo-Jo. I am sixteen years old and I'm a runaway.

What did I run away from? Well, not much. A year ago, a dead-end children's home in dead-end downtown Birmingham. Sophie and I ran away one Friday afternoon because first, we'd had enough of being told what to do and second, sixty quid had gone missing from the petty cash and someone had put the finger on Sophe. Sophie looked at me, and I knew what she was going to say. She'd run away before and she was on a warning. One more incident, they'd said, and she would be sent to a secure unit, whatever that was. She dreaded it, that's all I knew. We could stay and fight it; but Sophe and me had been in so much trouble recently we knew they wouldn't believe a word we said.

We'd all been asked to gather in the day room. The police were due in half an hour.

'Jo-Jo. Let's run away.'

I was scared, I don't mind saying. It was true I was sick of it all; sick of being told what to do; sick of getting the blame for every tiny thing, guilty or not. But *running away*? I'd imagined it – dreamt about it. But now it was too real.

We'd talked through a plan before. Sophie had a half-sister living in London, and we'd always said this was where we'd go, if it ever came to it. She would put us up, let us live there, even.

There was a hollow where my stomach should have been. I was terrified of both situations – staying and going. It was a split-second decision.

'I'm going *anyway*,' said Sophe, shoving stuff into her rucksack. 'You have to decide now! What's it gonna be, Jo-Jo. Now or never?'

Life would have been unbearable without Sophe and

anyway, they'd probably have accused me too, as her accomplice or something, and *I'd* have been the one in the secure unit.

So next thing, we were on the train. We'd had just enough to buy two child singles. 'Wow, Sophe!' I said, gasping, shaking.

We sat, breathless, looking at each other, hardly believing what we'd done. Then we suddenly started giggling, we couldn't help ourselves, and all the terror I'd felt just seemed to dissolve. We'd done it. We were free! I was thinking, it would be OK, wouldn't it? After all, we were going to Sophie's *sister.*

I couldn't have been more wrong.

Dark, dank steps from the street into this basement well, the walls covered in moss. A battered door with no bell. We had to knock and knock. Sophie's sister was still in her nightie, even though it was half-past four! And she didn't look any too pleased to see us either, I can tell you. The place was an absolute *tip.* It stank of fags and something sweet and sickly – mould, I think – and the kitchen sink was piled high with washing-up; the bin overflowing. She said we ought to go back. She didn't want the police coming round. But Sophie *begged* her not to call the home. She spun some tale about us being beaten up, bullied, that's why we'd run away. It was quite a performance. Oscar-winning I'd say, because the sister – Marie – seemed to soften a bit and said, 'OK, just for tonight then. We'll see what to do in the morning.'

I was thinking, It's *not* OK for tonight, or any night. We were in this boxroom on a filthy mattress with no sheets and just a stinking single duvet between us. And it was rotten cold and I was thinking that it was probably the worst night of my life; and the biggest mistake of my life too.

I lay there in the dark; eyes wide open. I know Sophie was awake too. She'd been trying to pretend all this was fine; just because it was her idea; and her fault too, when you thought about it.

'You didn't take that money, did you, Sophe?' It just came out. I think I needed someone to blame.

Suddenly she was bolt upright, practically shouting at me. 'Jo-Jo, I thought you were my *friend*. I told you I never took it. Full stop.'

'Yeah, *but* . . .' I couldn't help myself.

'Yeah, but *what*? We're here, aren't we? We've escaped.'

'But Sophe . . . it's *awful*.'

'Well, it's all we've got. And we can't go back. We'll both be sent to some rubbish place. Locked up. Do you want that? *Do you?*'

I burst into tears. It was pathetic. I knew really I was half to blame. I just didn't want to admit it. And I was angry with her because I'd imagined this nice, friendly sister in a warm, clean flat and this rubbish pit was the end of the world as far as I was concerned.

I'm not a bad person. Really I'm not. I've just had a lot of things happen to me. First my mum disappears. Woke up one morning and she's gone. No note. Nothing. Can't even remember how old I was. Eight or something. And Dad couldn't look after me properly. Neighbour came round one day and found me on my own, trying to light the gas fire. She went ballistic and called in Social Services. Next thing I know, I'm in a children's home and my dad has disappeared too. Then foster homes, one after the other. Never worked out. I was always too 'angry', they said. They were all rubbish, anyway. And then I ended up in Deerhaven. Haven! I could laugh. But there was Sophie, my roommate. Red hair, mad curls. Cheek like you'd never believe. Tough. We became wild. The terrible two, they called us. And then we started bunking off school and the trouble started. We just weren't into being told what to do. That's all.

In the end, Sophie's deadbeat sister Marie (and her boyfriend Pete) let us stay. Except after a week or so she said we had to pay. Had to contribute to the household. Some household.

And Sophe says, 'But how can we do that? We're too young to work, and we can't give our real names, anyway.'

And Marie says, 'Do what I did. Beg. Get out there. Two young kids like you – people'll feel sorry for you. I'll tell you where all the best pitches are.'

And that was the start of it. I suppose we could have gone. Dunno where. Somewhere might have taken us without too many questions. But by then we had a good reason to stay. Paddy. Our dog. Pete's dog, really, although Pete would have let him starve to death if it was up to him. Someone gave him to Pete and he swanned around for a couple of days – look, I'm so cool with this dog – and then couldn't be bothered with him. He was a cross collie – black and white with the stupidest face you ever saw. But he was *gorgeous*. So me and Sophe took him over. Bought his food, kept him clean. Let him sleep on our bed. And from day one, when I was out on the streets, I took him with me.

A few weeks later, Sophie disappeared. One night she just didn't come home. It was dead cold and I was frantic. Marie didn't want to report it: 'We don't want the police nosing around, do we?' I was furious. How could she not even care!

Next day I went looking for her. Word on the street was that she'd been picked up by the police. I couldn't believe it. Stupidly, it only just then occurred to me that they'd be looking for us. The runaways. She was probably back at the home by now. Or worse – locked up in that secure unit she dreaded so much. Poor Sophe! She was my only real friend, apart from Paddy. I prayed that she wouldn't give me away. But somehow I knew deep down that she wouldn't. And I was terrified that Marie would chuck me out. And what about Paddy? What would he do then?

So I just kept quiet; became helpful. That was the way to do it. Did washing-up and stuff, made them tea. As long as I kept out of the way and brought the money in, I was OK. But I can tell you for nothing that I was going downhill. Didn't eat much. Hardly changed my clothes. Living in that house with those two ate into your bones and changed you until you became exactly like them. I never really felt part of the human race and it wasn't hard to go the whole way, over the other side. And it was on a day I was feeling my worst that it happened. That magic day.

I set up my pitch, down a bit from the tube, by the river. It's a good spot to catch people on their way to work – people with money. I've got this sign: 'HELP ME, I'M HOMELESS.' I stick it in front of my knees. I find kneeling the best position. You don't look so rough.

This particular morning, I'm feeling a bit sick – I think I

was hungry – and I'm getting settled in my place with my filthy blanket and my money box, Paddy fussing around my ankles, when I suddenly feel faint. I *am* going to faint, and I lean back against the wall, feeling like a wind is blowing round my brain, sucking at it – and I am sliding down the wall when I feel a hand grab my upper arm and I'm thinking, It's got to be the police, for no one, no ordinary person would touch me, I'm so dirty and ragged – and then I start to focus, as I come back from the swoon. 'Are you OK?' There are these eyes looking at me. Deep brown eyes full of light, full of *concern*. No one had ever cared that I was OK since I can't remember when. And he's talking now, saying, 'Hey, sweetheart, sit down, take some deep breaths . . .' and he's gently supporting me, as I slide to the ground. And I'm looking up into his face, framed by short, dark curls, and those eyes – all the time those beautiful, clever eyes, telling me that he cares about me, truly he does. The face of an angel.

'Nice dog,' he says, patting Paddy's head. Paddy was going crazy with the attention. Wagging his tail off. Dogs know. They know the good from the bad.

That was the beginning of it. I suppose that, even then, you could call it love.

I'd never had a boyfriend. Told myself I wasn't interested. But really it was because I could never let myself believe that anyone could like me, ever. When you're in care, people treat you differently. It's like you're not part of the real world. Not even human.

But now I was thinking about him. That boy. A simple enough thing, except it wasn't. Normally, all I thought about every waking second was how to get enough cash to get food for Paddy and to keep Marie and Pete happy at the same time; or how I could somehow find Sophie. But now as I walked home, my pockets jangling with pennies (mean, mean – people are so *mean,* I'd be lucky if I'd made a fiver today), I was thinking about *him*. And, already, I was feeling sad because he was probably just passing by that morning, and I would never see him again.

I'd given up looking in the mirror. Why bother? I knew I was dirty, thin, scrawny – like something from a horror movie. But the next morning, I dared myself to have a proper look. And I did it oh-so-slowly, walking to the cracked mirror in the bathroom with my head down, and then slowly lifting my head – so I could just see my eyes. Sunken, pale eyes, and then my nose, my mouth – my lips all cracked and dry. Living here, like this, was like living underground; not in the real world. You weren't part of the human race. It was like you weren't able to breathe properly, always gasping for air.

But that morning, I forced myself to look. Surprisingly, my skin was sort of clear and my hair, although filthy, was still thick and curly. I might have been pretty, I thought. Was I?

And I washed my hair! Something I hadn't done in weeks. Washed it under the freezing tap water. As I towel-dried it, I felt my scalp tingle with the shock of being clean.

And there I was again. With my sign, 'HELP ME. I'M HOMELESS', watching, watching. I thought I'd break with the strain of watching. And every so often I'd see some young guy emerge and for a second I'd think, Is it him?

But that morning, the only thing that had happened was the woman from the centre with her stupid smile – Maggie, her name was – coming by. 'How are you, Jo-Jo?' She looked at me, her face serious.

And she bends down, talking softly about how they can help me . . . I'm so young . . . they've helped so many . . . I just have to take that first step . . . And I take her card and nod as if to say, Yeah, good idea, when she says I can call her any time, no questions asked. Pigs might fly. She gives Paddy a pat. He backs off. He's not sure of her at all. He lays down and puts his head in my lap. Protective.

Then lunchtime, as usual, Paddy and I go to the riverbank and sit with the others. Kids, vagrants, drop-outs. We share bits of food. I ask if anyone has heard from Sophie. No one has. No one cares, anyway.

Back on my pitch, early in the hot, sticky afternoon, I'm drowsy and just feeling as if I'm going to nod off when something makes me look up.

'You OK, now?'

I think I'm dreaming. He's just standing there. He's got a coffee and a sandwich and he's looking down at me with that look. I wish I could stand up, but I can't. I'm frozen to the ground. I run my hand through my hair and feel the surprise of its silkiness. I look back at him, into his eyes. I feel as if I will melt into the ground.

He's wearing jeans with a T-shirt and a linen jacket. It's like someone from another universe has spoken to me.

'It's just that you looked so pale – yesterday, I mean—'

'I'm OK, thanks . . .'

He's looking at me again. Looking at me in *that way.* If only I was some other person, in some other time, some other place; anyone but this filthy mess called Jo-Jo.

'Hey, have this . . .' he says, handing me his coffee. 'I've just had one.'

'No, no . . . 's OK, really.'

43

'Go on!' he says, putting it down on the ground beside me. 'You need it more than me.'

Paddy is all excited again. He's wriggling around, trying to get attention.

'Great dog,' he says, patting him. 'What's his name?'

'Paddy.'

Then he gives me a five-pound note! 'Buy him a bone or something.'

And then he was gone. I stood up, so I could see better, and watched him until he reached the junction and turned the corner. I felt like shouting after him.

The note crinkled in my hand. Five quid in one go! I felt like a millionaire. I put it in my sock. There was no way Marie and Pete were getting this money. I'd get stuff for Paddy.

The next day I was on edge, watching.

He didn't come.

He will come; he's got to come . . . whirled round and round in my head. Then, *He's not coming, he's not coming, he's not coming* . . . That I might never see him again, might never learn anything more about him, was unbearable. I am *so* stupid! I should have followed him to see where he went. I determined then, that if I ever got another chance . . .

That's how, next day, I found myself walking, like a shadow, ten metres or so behind him, my heart banging in my chest with nerves, and happiness. He'd come back. At the corner, he turned as before and swept down Baker's Walk and then left into a little alley. It was a narrow, cobbled street, with houses and offices that looked like they'd once been workshops or garages. I watched carefully: one, two, three, four – he entered the fifth door on the right. Blue, is it blue? Yes, the blue one. That was easy to remember. Once I was sure he was safely inside, I walked up to see if there was anything on the door. There was a silver plaque: ZOOT DESIGN. I wondered what he did in there. Design things, I supposed. It made me a bit sad. I mean, he was in the real world, doing stuff. And where was I? Underground, doing nothing.

And so it went on. Almost every day he came by and he'd smile and sometimes say, 'Hi there, OK?' and occasionally he'd bring me a coffee. And when he didn't come – off sick, on holiday . . . I could never know – I felt devastated. Completely and utterly. And if a few days passed without seeing him, this deepened to panic – would he come back, ever? It was unbearable.

One night in late summer, I was up near the station with some of the riverside gang. It was past eleven before I realised, with horror, that I hadn't fed Paddy. He'd be going crazy. It wouldn't occur to Marie or Pete to open a tin. Too much trouble. I took a shortcut through the little maze of streets that brought you out to the bus stop on the main road.

Just then, I realised I was in the street where *he* worked, and I felt a shiver rush through me. I looked at the blue door, ZOOT DESIGN, and then up at the windows which were black and shining with reflected light. The words of some old musical song came into my head, '*On the street where you live* . . .' For a few seconds the whole street seemed made of fairy dust. Then I headed on, turned left and, disbelieving, I saw him coming towards me – head down, hands in pockets, striding forward. *Was* it him? I couldn't believe my luck! The rolling walk, the dark curly hair. My heart was pounding.

And then suddenly, from nowhere, like something in a

film, the screech of brakes – a car – three lads jumping out – the car door flailing. For a second, I couldn't figure it out. Then the shock. A scuffle, a flash of steel, so quick. Even in my state, tired, confused – I felt the force of those lads, their heads wired up to nothing but what they were about to do. And I saw, as he turned, that it *was* him, his lovely face shocked and confused, although he was trying to fight back, to shove them off.

I don't know where it came from; somewhere deep, deep down inside, but a wild energy catapulted me forward; I shot at them like a bullet from a gun.

'Stop it! Stop it!'

By now they had him face down on the ground. There was blood. One of the lads looked round at me, his eyes wild, not registering. He thrust me out of the way. *Thwack!* I hit the pavement hard.

'Get his wallet. *Get it!*'

I was pulling myself up. As fast as they had come, they were gone. All I could hear was the noise of the car, brakes screeching, as it hurtled down the tiny, dark street.

Heart pounding, I turned him over. My angel. He was unconscious, his face covered in blood. Oh, God! What to do? Be OK. Be OK. And just looking at his face, I was making a prayer. Dear God, I was saying inside my head – although I had never prayed before – if you let him live, I will get away. I'll get away from this life and get myself together – make myself good. Good enough for him.

I promised this on his life.

I looked wildly around for a phone booth. Nothing. I had a hazy thought that I had passed a row of booths a couple of streets back.

I covered him with my jacket. I ran back up the cobbled street and round the corner. Was it this street? No, the next one – and thank God – a phone booth at the end of the road. Please be working.

I dialled 999. 'Ambulance! Someone has been hurt, mugged. My name? Doesn't matter. Hurry! Hurry! He's in England's Walk . . .' I could hardly speak. 'He's *bleeding*! Please, come quickly.'

And then I tore back. As I turned into the corner, two girls were running towards him. I stopped. One of them went forward and knelt down. She felt his pulse, she looked into his eyes. The other stood there, pulling out her mobile phone. *But I've already called*, I wanted to scream. *They're on the way . . . I've* taken care of him . . .

I wanted to push them out of the way, to look after him, like he'd looked after me. Then I glanced down at myself, my filthy clothes, my split trainers; ran my fingers through my tangled hair. You could see what I was. A street kid. A vagrant. I looked at them. It was so pathetic, but I didn't want those girls judging me. They'd probably think I had something to do with it. I couldn't risk the police coming.

Come on! Come on! Where is that ambulance?

I thought I would go mad with worry and frustration.

At last, the siren and the ambulance came crashing down the street. One of the girls got up, waving and jumping up and down. 'Here! Here!'

I watched, peeking round the wall. The other one – dark hair, red jacket, the girl who had felt his pulse – got up.

'He's got a nasty stab wound in his chest. His pulse is not bad, but he needs . . .'

The ambulance man kneeled down to check him out

while the stretcher was brought. 'Spot on,' he said. 'You done this before?'

'I'm a nurse at St Thomas's. Is that where he's going? I'll come with him. I don't mind.'

'*I'm a nurse!*' I mimicked. I couldn't help myself. I felt hatred welling up inside me. *I* was the one who'd saved him; *I* was the one who called the ambulance.

I watched as they carefully lifted him onto a stretcher. I watched the whole time, until the ambulance, with the two girls inside, sped off, siren shrieking. I walked to the place where he had been. I could still feel him there. The heat of his body. There was something black, crumpled in the gutter. My jacket. Kicked aside like an old rag. It wasn't even good enough to wrap him in.

I picked it up and ran, jumping on the first bus that came along. I was shaking all over. And worrying, worrying about *him*. And underneath it all, the promise I'd made running through my mind.

I'd even forgotten about Paddy. As soon as I walked through the door, he leapt at me, quivering all over, excited, loving, hungry. 'Paddy, boy!' I knelt down and hugged him. Fumbling, I got his food from the secret stash I'd bought with my little windfall. Then I sat down and tried to calm myself. Waiting until I could pick up the phone without shaking. I got the number from directory enquiries. St Thomas's Accident and Emergency. Please, please. Please be OK.

'I'm calling about a boy, a mugging – in Waterloo – about an hour ago. Is he OK? I just need to know.'

'Are you a relative?'

'No, it's just that I saw it. I called the ambulance.'

'Well, we can't really . . .'

'Oh, *please*. I don't need to know any details. Please, just that he's OK. *Please.*'

'Well, hang on . . .'

The wait was torture. I almost didn't want to know, just in case it was bad news. Then she was back.

'He's stable. That's all I can tell you.'

'You mean – he's OK– he's not going to die?'

'Well, maybe OK isn't the right word, but his life is not in danger. Now, hang on, please. You said you were a witness. The police want to talk to you. What's your name?'

I was almost swooning with gratitude. Thank you, God. Thank you, God! For a second I had forgotten the woman on the line.

'Hello, hello . . .' she was saying. 'You must hang on for the police. Who are you?'

'Nobody,' I said, and put down the phone.

It was the hardest thing I'd ever done in my life. That'll seem odd to you. To escape from that low-down life; from that filthy house – from Marie and Pete. But you have to understand. It was all I had. It may not have been much of a life, but it was my only life. A roof over my head, a bed. I had nowhere else to go. But I had made a promise, that night, when I held *him* in my arms. I was going through with it. Whatever it cost.

It was pitch black. I lay awake for ages, fully dressed, stroking Paddy's head. He was awake too, as if he knew. I had to do it that night. If I left it until morning, everything would be back to 'normal' again. My sad little routine, tea in bed for Marie and Pete, the street, my pitch outside the station. I would lose my nerve.

I must have lain there for over an hour, getting up the courage. Then I slid out of bed, like a shadow, picked up my bag, moved to the door and I peered out. I crept down the corridor, so, so slowly. 'Shh! Shh! boy. We need to be quiet. We're going out, OK?' I opened the door and we ran out into the night.

'What's your name, love?'

'Jo-Jo.'

'Jo-Jo who?'

'Jo-Jo Smith.' It was ridiculous, Smith. I could have laughed, if I hadn't been so scared.

'Where are you from, love?'

'Nowhere.'

'Well, look, we've got to have an address, if we're going to help you.'

Paddy was jumping around my heels, drawing attention to himself.

'I've got this.' I handed her the scrunched-up card I'd got from that woman from the centre. *Maggie Ellis – St Martin's Hostel.*

Maggie was called. 'It's fine. I know her.' She looked at me. 'I glad you came, Jo-Jo. But we can't take the dog.'

'Then I'm not staying.' I turned to go. I didn't know what I was going to do, just die probably – but I wasn't leaving Paddy.

'Wait. OK. Well, just for tonight, then.'

*

Three weeks later I was still there, and so was Paddy. I'd been through the mill. What was I on? Drugs, alcohol? I could see why they thought that, the state of me.

'I'm not on anything.'

She looked at me, disbelieving.

'I don't eat much.'

I had to be examined by a doctor. Have blood tests. To be sure I wasn't lying. I was clean, of course. But they didn't give up. Where are you from? Who *are* you?

'Jo-Jo Smith,' I said.

They looked me up everywhere. Scouring the world of missing girls. No Jo-Jo Smiths anywhere, of course. Anyway, I was sixteen; the Social Services would have given up. I didn't really exist in the real world.

That first night, I held Paddy in my arms. 'We've done it, boy! We've done it *for him.*'

Now I had to start the business of becoming a human being. And that was the second hardest thing I'd done in my life.

I became a good girl. I helped around the hostel. The food was rubbish, but I ate it – all of it. Within a week I had put on half a stone.

Then, when they thought I was ready, Paddy and I were moved to a halfway house. I suppose they meant halfway between being nobody and someone. That first night I had the longest bath ever, scrubbing myself clean. I looked in the mirror – properly, this time – not the usual, quick, sideways glance. And as I rubbed at the mist with a towel, I saw this face appear and it looked like, well, a normal person. Except something in my eyes – like there was a story there – a whole book of stories. My cheeks were round and my skin pink and white. My wet hair was wisping into curls, and I let it dry like that. I remembered my name, my real name. Joanna. That's who I'd been once, a long, long time ago when I was in a family, my family, and at school.

I thought of *him*, his face, the way he walked, and the way he said, 'Are you OK?' and that look, and I felt a sudden rush of something through my bones, as if my whole body was crying out with joy. Love, that's the only way I can say it.

But I knew enough to know I wasn't quite ready yet. I wasn't a hundred per cent human. I needed a job, something to make me part of the real world, his world.

One day, when I was up in my room, our social worker Patti yelled up the stairs. 'Down here, everyone! You've got a new housemate.'

Funny, I knew it before I even turned the corner. I felt this tingling in my fingers. The red hair, crazy as ever.

'Sophieeeeee!'

We couldn't believe it, neither of us. We screeched like two wild animals. She was just the same, but taller, skinnier.

'Have I been through it,' she said. 'Detention centre, the lot. I'm on probation now. But . . .'

I was laughing inside, to see her again. She was like my only family. My sister. 'Sophe, wait . . .'

I ran down the corridor and opened the back door. Paddy came careering down the hall like a bullet.

He knocked her down, licking her all over. 'I just can't believe it!' Sophie laughed. 'He remembers me.'

That night we told each other our stories.

We laughed so much we thought we'd explode. It was like the old days, only it wasn't. We were never going back there, if we could possibly help it.

I've got a job now. I walk there in the early afternoons. The other day I realised I was beginning to notice things, like trees and flowers, the sky, and the way the light changed. I work on the ticket box in a cinema and Paddy and me, we've got a room of our own. A bedsit, on the ground floor, with a french door opening onto a tiny garden. Sophe has to stay at the halfway house until she's finished her probation, but then she's going to come and live with us. Meanwhile, there's something I've got to do.

I've seen him lots of times. I go to Waterloo, to his street, taking a long way round so as to avoid my old hangout. The first time, I wondered what I'd feel, but it was just the same, as soon as I saw his face, the way he moved. I've followed him too. I've followed him at lunchtime and I've even followed him home. He lives not too far from me in a first-floor flat. One night, I stood across the road for maybe an hour, just watching. I know where he goes at lunchtime; and I know that on Saturday mornings he goes to the gym at the sports centre. I've been there, twice. There's a pool, with a big glass window that looks over the gym. I borrowed a swimming costume from Maggie, and risked it. The first plunge, well, it felt so good – that long-forgotten feeling of water, like silk, streaming over my body. How long had it been since I'd swum? I spent a lot of the time sitting on the edge of the pool, opposite the window, watching him – doing weights, the walking machine, that earnest, concentrating expression on his face.

I love him.

The second time I left the pool early, and waited, sitting on the benches in the corridor. I watched him come out of the gym, hair wet and curling from the shower, and go into the canteen. He passed me, sitting there pretending to read a magazine. I wasn't sure, but I think he looked twice. My heart turned over. But he wouldn't recognise me, would he? It was so important that I met him properly – as me – Joanna. And I could only pray that he wouldn't remember who and how I was. Although I think that would be hard, the way I am now. Blooming, Maggie says.

And this morning, Saturday again, I knew it was time. I woke up feeling the weight of my arms, the softness of my skin, as if life had been gradually seeping back into my body. I felt alive again. I fed Paddy, talking to him. 'Paddy boy, I'm going to meet our friend again. The one who gave us that fiver! Wish me luck.'

I got ready, oh, so carefully, and brushed my hair so it fell all around my face in bouncing curls. I put on my new jeans and the nice red top with the hood that Maggie had given me for my birthday. I didn't know exactly how I was going to do it; I just knew, with utter certainty, that there was something between us, something huge, and it had been there since that first time he had stopped and said, 'Are you OK?' I had done this thing, and it was all for him. I had saved my life.

*

I was so worked up, terrified, as I went into the sports centre. I didn't know if I was afraid he *wouldn't* be there, or that he *would* – and then I'd have to go through with it.

I swam, very briefly, and then sat on the edge of the pool, watching. And then he came! In his red shorts and black T-shirt. My heart was turning over and over.

I swam a little while longer, then stood up and shook myself, trying to shake some courage into my bones. The timing had to be exactly right. I couldn't miss, not now I had made up my mind. Everything seemed quiet and buzzy and I realised that I was half-paralysed with fear. I didn't know exactly what I was going to do. I could only pray that he didn't change his routine – that he'd go to the canteen like last time. I went into the changing room. I had a shower, washed my hair, and made up my face. It was Joanna who looked back at me. Jo-Jo had gone. I was ready.

He was sitting at one of the long tables. At once, I saw how it could go. I fetched a tray. I hardly know what I chose.

'Anyone sitting here?'

He smiled, and gestured to the chair. 'No, help yourself.'

I don't know how I kept myself calm. He was so close, I could have reached out and fallen into his arms.

'Excuse me? Do I know you?'

'Sorry?'

'Sorry, it's just that you look familiar . . .' He put his head on one side, thinking. I could have melted.

'Oh, I've come here a few times.'

'Hm, that's probably it, then–' he looked quizzical '– but . . . never mind.'

I smiled.

He smiled back. 'What's your name?'

'Joanna.'

'Hi, Joanna – I'm Jude.' He reached out to shake my hand. It was like a bolt of electricity through my arm.

The background noise seemed to disappear; the people too. There were just the two of us. We began to talk. About his job, about my job, and whatever there was on that first day was still there, only stronger than ever. He leant towards me and I felt true happiness, for the first time in as long as I could remember. Probably ever.

Then suddenly he looked up. His face changed. He smiled that smile, but in a different way; his whole body poised – his eyes full of light. My heart began to pound. *Bang, bang, bang.*

'Alice! You made it.'

A tall, dark-haired girl was walking over to our table. Everything was completely silent now. I felt a rush of blood to my face. This Alice was looking at me, questioning.

'Oh, hey, Alice – this is – sorry – what's your name again?'

'Joanna–'

Alice sat down while he went to fetch her a drink. She wouldn't look at me. She knew.

And then he was back. I was burning up inside. Wordlessly, every fibre of my being was shrieking, 'Please don't say it . . .'

But he went on. 'Yeah, Alice is my fiancée. If it hadn't been for her, I'd be dead. Really. But, hey, that's another story . . .'

I knew then. *I'm a nurse at St Thomas's. I'll come with him. I don't mind.*

It should have been me. I was the one who saved him. How could this go so terribly wrong?

I woke up the next morning feeling completely dead. Empty. Paddy jumped on my bed and snuggled up. He knew something bad had happened. He always knew. But this time, he couldn't comfort me. Nothing could. I made some tea, sat at the table and stared out the window. What had it all been for? I re-ran the scene again and again. *My fiancée . . . Alice.* But there *had* been something between us. It was still there. How could he not feel it? I felt the world crashing around me.

I rang Sophie. 'Can you come, *please*.'

'Now?'

'Yes, now.'

An hour later Sophie blustered through the door. I couldn't believe how much I had missed her. She'd bought us doughnuts and tea from the café on the corner. We sat at my tiny table.

Shaking, I told her the story – everything. She listened, wide-eyed.

'A nurse!' she shrieked. 'How could you expect to compete with a *nurse* saving his life . . .? Just your luck – angels, they call them, don't they? She's probably a stupid prissy cow, anyway.' She pulled her 'I've got something nasty under my nose' face. She was so funny I wanted to laugh.

And I did. Real laughter. It rose up from my stomach in great waves, and it felt so good . . . and then I cried. It was like a dam bursting.

What was it all for? I felt as if I'd been emptied out of any feeling I'd ever had. Then for weeks I felt nothing. Nothing at all. Then one day I woke up and felt OK. I mean I wasn't underground any more, struggling for breath. I had a room, a job; I had Sophie and Paddy. I was living in the world, and I suppose I had him to thank for that.

This story was inspired by 'The Little Mermaid'. CC

The Flames of Love

The red Peugeot thudded down the green lanes, tearing a path of raw sound through the still evening that followed a hot June day. Three of the four boys, including the driver, Rich, bounced around in their seats to the loud music. The fourth, Jon Tinner, clutched his seat-belt nervously, a stiff grin plastered to his face and his eyes squeezed shut behind the wraparound sunglasses. Each poorly judged bend that forced him to see in close-up the frothy cow-parsley at the side of the road flashed him back to the motorbike accident ten years earlier. For him the fine white tracery of those flowers spelt pain and blood, gave off the stench of hot oil and metal and torn flesh.

Jon didn't know where they were. They must have driven at least twenty miles out of the city to this party. It was one way of celebrating the end of exams, he supposed, going to this mystery party with his mates. Better than the manly drink in the pub his father had proposed.

Jon had heard a lot about Amy Rossiter – Rich's ex – and the house in the country, with ponies and a pool, that was practically a palace. He'd seen a wide-angle snap of Amy on Rich's mobile but it could have been anybody. In fact, Rich was scrolling through for it with his left thumb right now, as he negotiated the right-hand turn on to the main road. He barely registered the petrol tanker hurtling towards them.

'Watch out!' shrieked Gaz, and all four of them ducked instinctively. Jon flew through the air as if in a dream, ruby-red droplets of blood spattering the white lace flowers where he landed. An agonising pain seared through his left thigh.

Jon opened his eyes fearfully. It was all right. His memory had been playing tricks again. He was still in the car. The petrol tanker was already in the distance. The ridged web of ugly scarring on crushed thigh was old and hidden under his jeans. Jon took a deep breath. Several deep breaths.

Rich and the others were laughing nervously. 'Idiot!' Rich leant on the horn for the benefit of the retreating petrol tanker and jabbed his foot down on the accelerator. 'Not far now – ten miles max,' he said to his passengers. 'Hold tight!' Jon shrank down in his seat and shut his eyes again. The others were loving the ride, pumped up by the thrill of danger – why wasn't he? How was such a coward ever going to cope with the jungle trekking he had planned for next year?

Amy's house had a long, gravel driveway. 'Slow down, Rich,' said Gaz, alarmed by the spurting stones. 'Don't want to mow down the talent.' He lowered his window and stuck his head out to admire the girls in their party silks darting down the driveway like dragonflies over a river. 'Posh totty,' he remarked. A boy in a tuxedo stepped out to direct them to a parking space in the paddock. Rich pulled up on the grass. The four boys climbed out of the Peugeot, their scruffy clothes crumpled from the journey. 'Perhaps this wasn't such a good idea,' said Gaz, catching the scent of the canvas marquee and crushed grass and class.

''Course it was,' said Rich. 'Amy won't mind that we're not dressed up. Bunch of fit lads like us.' He nonchalantly removed his baseball cap and chucked it on the back seat before locking the car and pocketing the keys. He grinned at Jon. 'Apart from our mate Tinner, of course.'

Jon limped alongside them; he was accustomed to this heavy-handed humour.

'Sorry, mate,' added Rich unapologetically. 'Now where's Amy? You can always spot her a mile off. She has that dancer's walk.'

Jon spotted her simply because she was beautiful. His senses were still adjusting to the fading light and the scent of the syringa that spilled over the garden, when she emerged from amongst the white flowers: an English rose, with long, silky, light brown hair, charcoal eyelashes and a blushing complexion. Not tall, wearing a dress the same soft colour as the twilight. A heart-shaped gold locket gleamed at her throat. She didn't have a dancer's walk. How could she, with crutches?

Jon gazed at Amy as she swung herself towards them. His heart turned over. 'She's like me,' was the thought that crackled through his brain. 'She knows. She knows how it feels to be damaged, to be different.' And he felt his eyes misting over as he looked at a twin soul. He was standing stock still, his head on one side, as Amy approached. She caught his scorching glance for one long, heart-stopping moment, but before Jon could believe it had happened she launched herself at Rich.

'Rich!' she squealed. '*What* are you wearing? It's my eighteenth! Didn't you read the invite? *Can* you read?' She looked coolly at Jon and Gaz and Jamie. 'Which part of "admit one" didn't you understand?' Jon, Gaz and Jamie shuffled their feet like small boys and mumbled their apologies.

But Rich dismissed all that. 'Come on, Amy, don't pretend you're not pleased to have more guys at your party! You know your girlfriends will be eternally grateful. And I've got my own car, now; I had to fill it, didn't I?' Amy looked interested. She liked boys with cars. 'Anyway, cripple,' Rich laughed, pointing at the crutches, 'what happened to you?'

Jon winced. *Cripple?*

'Do you even *open* my e-mails, Rich? I had an operation on my shin. It's a ballet thing. *So* painful, though. You might at least have sent a get-well card.'

'I'm sorry,' said Rich, chastened at last.

Amy seemed to forgive them. 'Go in the marquee and get yourselves something to eat and drink, guys. Any more gatecrashers like you and there won't be enough to go round!' From under her lashes she surreptitiously checked out the boy who had looked at her so longingly, before turning away with a lilting laugh and propelling herself towards some new arrivals, the perfect hostess.

Jon's friends threw themselves into the party and danced the night away, but Jon was drawn to Amy amongst the coloured lanterns like a moth to a candle. He hovered around her, but she didn't know him, didn't know his name, even. Once she sat down by him. He caught her scent, longed to touch her, longed to talk to her, but the music was too loud. Round about two in the morning he realised he was in love. He curled up under the coats and hugged the thought to himself.

Amy stayed in Jon's head, a cuckoo in his brain, elbowing out all other thoughts. Her silky hair, the dress fashioned from twilight and the fringe of dark lashes brushing her rose-petal cheeks, were with him constantly. The image of her shimmering dancer's body tormented him. All the while he prepared for his jungle adventure his soul yearned for its twin.

Because he was clever, and a quiet wit, Jon's lameness hadn't really been a problem at school. But now, sitting on the plane to Sarawak, aware of a throbbing ache from under the scarring on his thigh, he seriously wondered – a bit late in the day – if he was going to be able to keep up with the trek through the jungle that lay ahead. He determined to get strong and fit while he was out there, to strengthen the wasted muscles as much as he possibly could

Jon reminded himself of this as they climbed the first slopes. Back at the longhouse where his companions were mostly German and older than him, he climbed into his hammock, too tired to try and make conversation with people who couldn't understand him. His legs ached each night, but gradually, day by day, he felt them growing stronger.

Jon thought he might be able to rest up a bit when they set off down the river towards the caves, six to a raft, but he hadn't bargained for the countless times they had to get out and push the boat off the mud banks. With his strong arms he turned out to be one of the best at this, and his damaged leg didn't buckle as he'd feared. The underwater caving was terrifying. Jon's torch went out, and he had a few moments of sheer claustrophobic terror – afraid that the waters would rise or the roof would fall in, or both – as he sloshed about in the darkness, until the battery miraculously burst into life again.

Back in England, Amy's shin was not mending as it should. She had gone back to dancing too early and after that she was forced to spend the summer with her feet up. Reading on a beach was fine on holiday in Greece, and she was allowed to swim, but once home again time weighed on her. Unable to dance, ride, or even walk up and down the high street without crutches, Amy became more reflective than usual. She started to wonder how it would feel to be like this for ever. Her mind went back to the boy Rich had brought to her party. Had he always been like that, always limping behind the crowd? She wished she'd taken the opportunity to talk to him. And one day, as she lay in a hammock in the garden, drifting off in the dappled sunlight of a late summer afternoon, she suddenly recalled the penetrating look he had given her. Amy was used to boys looking at her, but this had been such an intense gaze. It had stayed smouldering with her all this time.

Amy asked her friends if any of them remembered the boy, one of the four who hadn't bothered to put on evening dress? None of them did. She e-mailed Rich, knowing he never answered e-mails, but she was surprised by an instant reply. Rich was bored, and pleased that Amy had contacted him. He didn't answer her question but, sensing that she didn't have a boyfriend, suggested that he came down to visit her. Reluctantly, Amy agreed. He roared up in the red car and bore her off to the local pub for lunch, where he proceeded to talk about himself. Amy tried to get the conversation round to the boy who had been with him that night. In the end she asked him outright.

'Gaz, you mean?' said Rich. 'Gaz is OK. Not your type though. Bit conventional.'

'I don't think he was called Gaz,' said Amy. 'Who were the others?'

'Can't think why you're interested,' said Rich, incapable of seeing that Amy could have eyes for anyone but himself. 'Jamie's a laugh. Quite nice-looking if you go for long-haired romantics, I suppose.'

'I don't think he was called Jamie either,' said Amy, puzzled that this was so difficult.

'Well, there wasn't anyone else,' said Rich, 'unless you count old Jon!'

'What do you mean? Why shouldn't he count?'

'He's just – well – he just isn't . . . as *fit* as most people.

Not like you. He doesn't do any of the things that you and I like doing. He can't drive, for a start. And he doesn't windsurf or play footy or anything physical like that.'

'Most people are fitter than me at the moment. Anyway, humour me. Tell me about him.'

'Jon Tinner? Had an accident on his father's motorbike when he was about eight, I think. Bit of a geek.'

'He's your friend. You must like him.'

'Yeah, I suppose so. He's quiet sometimes. He's got a very dry sense of humour. Drops a comment into a conversation and it takes everyone a while to realise that he's just said something really funny. Sticks at things.'

Amy began to like the sound of Jon Tinner. 'So where is he?'

'Gone trekking somewhere crazy. Borneo, I think.'

Only the orang-utans made the trekking bearable as far as Jon was concerned. Each morning in the jungle they woke up soaked. Leeches covered his legs as they walked through the swampy undergrowth. It was wild and beautiful, but very tough-going. Jon imagined Amy there. She seemed to dance ahead of him, like a will-o'-the-wisp. She drew him onwards. He wondered if she ever thought of him.

The final part of Jon's adventure gave him and his German companions time to relax on the beautiful beaches. Jon had learnt a few more German phrases by now, and most of the Germans spoke good English, he realised. One night he lingered over a driftwood bonfire with a young woman called Karin. She tossed her white-blond plait over her shoulder and questioned him. 'So, Jon. You have a girlfriend at home?' she asked.

'Not a girlfriend, no,' said Jon, staring into the firelight. 'But there's a girl I really like.'

'She should like you, too, no? You have courage. And you're not bad-looking!'

'Huh,' said Jon. 'Nice face, shame about the leg, you mean?'

'Sorry?' said Karin, not understanding.

'Well, I'm lame, aren't I?' said Jon.

'I had not noticed,' said Karin.

'You mean you hadn't noticed these scars?' said Jon, hitching up his shorts.

'No,' said Karin. 'Not until now!'

Jon smiled with pleasure, while his image of Amy leapt and pirouetted amongst the blue and orange flames of the fire on the sands.

Jon and Karin became good friends. She was several years older than him and their age difference took the pressure off them both, especially since Karin had a boyfriend back home. At one camp she and Jon took the Land Rover to fetch stores and she offered to teach him to drive. 'I'm not sure I can drive anything but an automatic, with my leg,' said Jon.

''Course you can,' said Karin. 'Shift over and have a go.' By the end of the beach week, Jon had become an adept driver. He didn't fancy his chances on the motorway or parking in a city street, but he could get from one place to another. And driving in the jungle was so different from being on the roads at home. The flashbacks stayed away.

Amy's condition was making her look differently at the world. She wondered if it made the world look differently at her. Did people feel sorry for her? Would she for ever be the dancer whose career was ruined? Did she care if it was, even?

By nature impulsive and quick, she was getting used to waiting, to moving more slowly. She became less judge-mental, looking at people she didn't know more carefully, and making up elaborate histories for them in her head.

Used to being popular, she had to learn not to mind when her friends took off without her. She couldn't dance, she couldn't windsurf, she could barely even shop! She read a lot. She found herself returning to Jon and his gaze – his loving gaze. She got into the habit of fiddling with the heart locket at her neck whenever she thought about him.

When Jon's parents met him at the airport they couldn't believe how fit and strong their son had become. He wanted driving lessons as a birthday present, passed his test before Christmas and had a job delivering motor parts – van included – by the New Year. Jon felt purposeful. He wanted to earn money, buy himself a car, be the sort of guy that Amy would be interested in. He hadn't tried to get in touch with her since his return, hadn't known how to. Anyway, it would have been crazy. He knew she must have forgotten all about him by now – probably had no memory of him at all. He hadn't seen Rich, either. Everyone was a bit vague about Rich.

Rich knew Jon was back and kept away. He felt strangely annoyed with him. It was all to do with Amy, of course. He didn't want to have to tell his old friend that Amy was interested in him, or tell Amy that Jon was home. He still wanted Amy for himself.

But Jon's heart had its own plans for him. It wanted to take him back to the place where he had fallen so hopelessly in love. It wanted to prove that love might not be so hopeless after all.

Jon bought his car one freezing day in January. He filled it up with petrol, said goodbye to his parents and set off to test it out. The car purred along. There wasn't much traffic about. It followed the remembered journey dictated by Jon's heart. Jon managed the right-hand turn on to the main road with no trouble at all. Down the lanes the hedgerows were furred with frost. A robin perched on a branch. It was beautiful. Jon's heart sang as his car brought him closer to Amy.

He found himself crawling along behind a horsebox for what seemed like miles. On an impulse he turned off as soon as he could, and followed the narrow lanes where they led. Here was a turn by a pub that felt familiar; a barn; an old-fashioned signpost in a grassy triangle, and then the gateway to Phoenix House. The name of Amy's house flew back to him. He had arrived at his heart's destination!

Jon steered cautiously up the gravel driveway. He had no idea what he was going to do beyond ringing on the doorbell, no plan at all.

Amy opened the door and clutched on to it, speechless, staring at Jon for a few seconds before throwing her arms around his neck. He hugged her so tightly that her feet left the ground. 'Put me down gently, Jon,' she whispered. 'I need something to hold on to these days. This leg's kind of useless.'

'Who is it?' Amy's mother called from deep inside the house.

'A friend of Rich's,' said Amy, smiling. 'He's going to drive me out to the pub.' She smiled brilliantly at Jon. 'Aren't you? Assuming you came in a car?'

Amy's mother appeared, tea towel in hand. She looked at Amy questioningly.

'It would take too long to explain, Mum,' said Amy impatiently, her eyes bright. 'But Jon arriving like this is completely magic. Just amazing. Bye!'

Jon couldn't believe the dream he was in. Amy was here! She loved him! As much as he loved her! He stopped the car at the end of the drive and they kissed.

Jon drove on to the road. The ice had taken a grip. The tea-coloured puddles were milky and frozen. Jon gazed into Amy's shining eyes before turning right on to the main road. He was on fire with happiness. He didn't see the petrol tanker hurtling towards them.

The bodies lay entwined amongst the white tracery of the frosted verge. Ruby droplets of blood decorated the shattered windscreen of the burning car. In the middle of the road lay Amy's heart locket, intact and gleaming.

This story was inspired by 'The Steadfast Tin Soldier'. KP

Mummy's Boy

Flora had secretly fancied Mark for ever. He was entirely fanciable, with thick, straw-coloured hair and dark-lashed, deep blue eyes. What's more, he had that way of *looking* at her, when he spoke to her, even though she was only one of his girlfriend's mates. And sometimes, when they talked together, she felt as if he really found her interesting; as if, given time, they could talk and talk into the night.

No, the problem with Mark, as his many ex-girlfriends attested, was his mother. Mark and his mother had a *big* mutual admiration thing going. His mother adored him, linked her arm through his and positively *paraded* her handsome son around the place. And the sickening thing was, Mark *went along* with it. He went along with it because he adored her back. Or seemed to. Flora had her own theories. Because Mark could do no wrong in her eyes, she reckoned that it was simply kindness on his part.

In all other respects, according to Chloë, Alice, Louisa and a good many others, Mark was OK. Genuinely OK. It wasn't just his pretty face. As a boyfriend he was known to be attentive and sexy and considerate – until his mother appeared on the scene, that was, and then he seemed to melt away. At first she would just offer coffee and girly chat, the girlfriends said. She'd stand there in the kitchen, laughing too much and joining in like mad. Then she would start to offer suggestions about clothes and beauty treatments. How a little eyebrow-shaping might not go amiss. Wouldn't pale colours suit your skin better than those vibrant ones? Hair worn *just so* would be so much more flattering to the bone structure . . . And before long, she was an integral part of the relationship, they told Flora. You weren't simply going out with Mark – you were going out with Mark and Janey (as Mark spookily addressed her). Janey claimed that she had so much fun with Markie's girlfriends. She would so much have loved a daughter of her own. And then you weren't going out with Mark at all. You'd been dumped. And it felt as though it was Janey who'd done the dumping.

Flora couldn't believe that Mark was the kind of boy who couldn't stand up to his mother. And deep down (in the way that we all rejoice *ever so slightly* in our best friends' failed relationships) Flora thought that perhaps his mother was right – none of her friends was quite the right one for Mark. Not in the way that *she* would be!

Mark freely admitted that he *was* looking for the perfect relationship. He believed in true love. The ex-girlfriends would wearily explain to Flora that he already had that with his mother, didn't he? Why bother looking any further? Or why didn't he simply let Janey do the choosing, since she seemed to know so much better than he did what he wanted in a girl? They were pretty sure that witchy old Janey was instrumental in ending each of their relationships with Mark.

'How?' asked Flora. She'd never actually met Janey face-to-face.

None of the girls could answer that question precisely. 'Something to do with staying over,' said Alice.

'I never got to stay at Mark's place more than once,' said Chloë.

'Nor me,' said Louisa. 'I almost felt as if I'd failed a test somehow.'

When Mark went off on his gap year, his mother was distraught. She had the kitchen redesigned. She spent a lot of time at the health club. Mark rang her every day at first, but as he went from the beaches of Thailand to the lush forests of Vietnam and on to the breathtaking altitudes of the Himalayas, his phone calls to her grew less frequent. Flora and her friends, still in their last year at school, passed by his suburban palace every day as the fallen leaves were rimed with frost, as Christmas lights shone wanly round the gates, as snowdrops and pale daffodils pushed up through the grass on the surrounding banks. Sometimes they spotted Janey in the distance and legged it, loath to be trapped into conversation by her. They had their own e-mails from Mark. They knew, each of them, how the world was treating him, and about the various beauties he had sadly rejected because they didn't quite match up to his ideal somehow.

*

Flora missed Mark dreadfully too, but in some ways it was easier to dream about him when he wasn't there; to imagine him being hers alone, when he wasn't going out with one of her friends. So she wasn't too downhearted. She also had exams to contend with, and UCAS forms, and a future to look forward to. And Flora – beautiful Flora, we should add, since Flora had long auburn curls and green-gold bright eyes, an athletic body and a sensible, intelligent demeanour – had many friends. She had older brothers who teased her and a baby sister who loved her, not to mention a doting dad and a marvellous mum – Flora was not in need of love; she was full of it.

Late one evening, when March winds battled with pelting April showers and shiny new leaves rattled and shook and dripped in the orange light of the streetlamps over her head, Flora was walking home alone in the dark. This was unusual. Usually Flora made sure that she walked home with Alice or Chloë or Louisa, but tonight had not been a good night. Gangly Jake had been making moves on her all evening and though Flora was fond of Jake and would never hurt him, she didn't fancy him at all. So she had slipped away from the loud music and the unwanted attention, and flitted home alone through the dark.

Except that she wasn't alone. The footsteps that dogged her own stopped when she stopped. When Flora ran, the footsteps speeded up. Flora looked around. Someone dodged behind a wet laurel bush. The dark stretches between the suburban villas grew longer. Flora stopped briefly under a lamppost to call home and ran on with her mobile held to her ear. No reply, and she hadn't the breath to leave a message. The electronic beeps and trills were comforting, but Flora knew that out there in the wind and the rain, someone was following her. Across a municipal rose garden, Flora recognised the security lights of Mark's house. If she sprinted, she could reach it safely before her stalker caught her up. Flora looked behind her. She caught a movement. She looked ahead at the wet pavement. She looked to the right across the rose garden to Mark's house. She decided to run.

Flora's heels sank into the grass. She kicked off her shoes and sped past the thorny rosebushes that snagged her clothes. She skidded and fell on the wet grass and picked herself up, her tights muddy. Whoever it was hadn't caught up with her. Flora pounded up the front path of Mark's house – it *was* Mark's, wasn't it? – and jabbed at the doorbell.

'Who is it?' bleated Janey's voice through the intercom.

'It's Flora,' she gasped. 'A friend of Mark's. I need help – I'm being followed!' she added breathlessly. 'Please can I come in?' The door buzzed and Flora fell into the house, Mark's house.

'It's very late,' said Janey, swaying, wine glass in hand, as Flora closed the front door and leant against it, still panting. 'Do I know you?' Janey asked, peering at the muddy and bedraggled young woman who stood dripping before her. 'You're lucky I let you in,' she said. 'You look as if you've been dragged through a hedge backwards.'

'I have,' said Flora, 'kind of. I told you – I was being followed, so I ran like crazy and I kept slipping over. I was really scared. Thank you for letting me in.'

'Do we need to call the police?' asked Janey, finally

showing a little concern as she led Flora down the steps to the redesigned kitchen.

'I think I'm safe enough here, thanks,' said Flora. 'I'm texting my parents to pick me up.'

'Well, you don't *look* like one of Mark's girlfriends, Flora – is it?' said Janey, peering over her glass before taking another sip. Mark's girlfriends were a well-groomed lot on the whole, but this one – well! Not much make-up, for a start, but what mascara there had been was running down her face, hair all over the place as she stabbed at her phone. It was hard to imagine her under normal circumstances.

Flora knew how dishevelled she must look but she gulped at Janey's rudeness. However, she didn't want to be thrown out by this drunken woman before she had contacted her parents. Her stalker might still be at large. 'Mark and I never actually went out together,' she explained, 'but I know Louisa and Chloë and Alice and the others. We're friends.'

'All pretty girls,' mused Janey. 'Not right for my Markie, but pretty, at least. Ah well, you'd better wait here and dry out. Are your parents on their way?'

'I'm sure they won't be long,' said Flora. 'I won't get in your way.' Just then, Flora's phone beeped and she checked for a text message. Janey looked at her expectantly, taking quick sips of her wine. 'Oh dear,' said Flora, sitting down weakly. 'That's a drag. They're staying over at Gran's. Mum wants me to go to a friend's house tonight . . .' She looked at her phone and its unwelcome news in dismay. 'Usually it's not a problem, it's just – it's just that my friends are all still at the club, and they won't be back until the small hours,' she wailed. Tears welled in Flora's eyes as she rang her mother back. 'Pick up, pick up . . .' she muttered desperately as there was no response. 'Reception's lousy where they are.' The bad night was getting worse.

'I suppose,' said Janey, 'I suppose . . .'

Flora wondered what was coming.

'I suppose I could make you up a bed here.'

Flora thought of the huge house she'd heard so much about. Surely it wouldn't be *that* much trouble. But she was utterly exhausted and any bed would be welcome.

'Thank you,' said Flora. 'I'm really tired. I'll leave first thing in the morning. I won't be a bother to you.'

'Wait here, then,' said Janey. 'It will take me a little while to get your bed ready.' And she staggered off upstairs. Flora could hear her moving around – heaving things around – while she called her brother's mobile to get him to ring Gran for her.

Janey came back into the living room, poured herself another drink, and exhaled noisily. 'It's all ready for you,' she told Flora. 'The room at the top of the second flight of stairs. It's got an ensuite. Sleep well.' And she concentrated on getting another glass of wine down her.

Flora picked up her bag, ready to go upstairs, but then she wavered. Janey looked so frail and pathetic – and lonely. 'What about you, Janey?' Flora asked kindly, touching her shoulder. 'Aren't you going to bed too?'

'I'll finish my drink,' said Janey. 'Don't want to waste it.'

'My mum always falls asleep on the sofa if she has too much wine,' said Flora, laughing. 'My dad has to shake her to wake her up.'

'Lucky old her,' said Janey. 'Goodnight, then.'

'Oh – I'm so sorry,' said Flora, wrong-footed. 'I wasn't

thinking.' She had no idea when Mark's dad had moved out.

'No, no. Mustn't be bitter. Too long ago for that.' Janey took another swig.

'You must miss Mark dreadfully,' said Flora. 'I'd hate to be in a house on my own.'

'I do hate being alone,' said Janey. 'It's not something you grow out of. But I've only myself to blame. And Mark has to live his own life, now. I know that.' Her shoulders shook and she gave a quick hiccough of a sob.

Flora's instinctive response to someone in tears was to hug them. Even if that someone was Janey. Flora couldn't help it. She threw her arms around Mark's mum and clasped the thin body briefly. 'Thank you again, Janey,' she said, moving away. 'It's really kind of you to let me stay. I was so petrified out there.'

'It's nothing,' said Janey. 'See you in the morning.'

Upstairs, Flora couldn't think why Janey had taken so long to prepare her room. It was a perfectly normal guest room as far as she could tell. It even had its own bathroom. Was there some sort of catch? Was there a pea lurking under the mattress, like in the fairy tale? Would she fail the test and ruin her chances with Mark before she ever got together with him?

Flora peeled off her muddy clothes and had a quick shower. Then she saw that Janey had laid out fresh towels and a clean nightie for her. There was a hot-water bottle in the newly-made-up bed, too. No wonder it had taken Janey a while to do all this, especially in her drunken state. Flora draped her wet clothes over the radiator before climbing under a sweet-smelling duvet and warming her toes on the hot-water bottle. She drifted off to sleep, still amazed that she was actually inside Mark's house and realising with a pang how much she was looking forward to his return.

Flora slept well. She got up and dressed before Janey appeared, and left her an effusive thank-you note on the kitchen table.

Two months later, when Flora had nearly finished her exams, Mark returned. He called Flora the very next day. 'Janey told me to ring you,' he said.

'Oh?' said Flora, dimly remembering that night *chez* Janey. 'Why?'

'She just went on about it. So, I thought – you know – anything for a bit of peace.'

'She looks out for you, does she? Your mum?' Flora was secretly thrilled. Had she passed the test somehow? Already?

'Do you want to come over? We could go out for a meal.'

'OK,' said Flora, trying to sound casual. 'Whatever.' As soon as she rang off she called Alice and Chloë and Louisa for emergency first-date help. All three arrived at Flora's house within minutes, armed to the teeth with clothes and make-up and eyelash curlers.

'Are you sure you want to do this?' asked Alice, stroking mascara on Flora's eyelashes.

'You'll have to deal with *Janey*, you know,' said Chloë, painting nail varnish on Flora's toenails.

'She'll want to talk to you all the time, and do stuff with you,' added Louisa over the noise of the hair-dryer as she dried Flora's hair.

Flora sat amongst her attendants like a princess. 'She's lonely,' she said simply. 'All on her own in that great big house.'

'Suit yourself,' the other three said in unison.

Flora waited for someone to open the door. She heard approaching footsteps and braced herself for seeing Mark.

And there he was, tanned and gorgeous. He hugged her like a friend, and she wanted it to go on and on. But it wasn't time yet. There was Janey close behind. 'Off you go, you two,' she said, surprisingly. She smiled. 'Don't want you hanging around here all evening. Go on, shoo! I've got things to do.'

'That's a first,' said Mark, when they were outside. 'Usually she makes me feel guilty for not inviting her along too.' He stood away from Flora and looked her up and down. 'You look great, by the way,' he added gruffly. 'Mum reminded me that you had something really special. She said you were different from other girls.'

'Steady on,' said Flora. But she couldn't help feeling pleased.

Mark reached for her hand. Flora felt the electricity leap between them and her limbs turned to liquid. But she wasn't going to make it all easy for him. 'So you needed Janey's approval, did you?'

'Sort of,' said Mark, squeezing her hand before lacing his fingers in hers. 'But I don't want to talk about her any more. I've got better things to bore you with.'

Flora allowed herself a quick sideways glance at the boy who was holding her hand. *Me*, she thought. *Me* with Mark. And it's just as I'd always hoped it would be. 'But *I* want to talk about her. I need to know,' she said out loud, 'what it was that made Janey think I was different.'

'OK, I'll tell you,' said Mark, turning to face Flora and resting his arms on her shoulders. 'You were the first person in a long time to treat her as a human being. And she said you gave her a hug. A spontaneous hug. She said–' Mark faltered '–she said she knew you were full of love, and that's the only sort of girl she wants for her son.'

And then Mark kissed Flora, and she kissed him back.

This story was inspired by 'The Princess and the Pea'. KP

The King of Cool

'How cool is *that*!'

Pete Ferris stood at his mirror giving it some serious full frontal. Yep, from the front, side, back – wow – you had to admit it. He looked cool from every angle.

His brand-new, top-of-the-range, just-on-the-market Iko jeans with the low-slung waistband and cool-cut leg just *slid* off his hips as if they'd been tailored by angels, exclusively for him. Quality, man! As usual he'd been watching, studying, the website – FUTURE TODAY – every day, practically every second, since he'd heard the new Ikos were about to come on the market. He'd spent hours on the Net trying to find someone jumping the gun with stock. But there seemed to be this embargo thing, whatever that was, which stopped people selling them early, before they were officially 'launched'. He'd been determined to be the first in Baybridge to get a pair. Admittedly, it wasn't too difficult in this backward, backwoods town, but you couldn't take any chances. So he'd spent twenty pounds of his precious clothing fund to go to London and queue all night (his mum had gone mad – but how could *she* possibly understand?) outside Sharks in Piccadilly where he'd been third in line and had come away swinging his ice-cool Iko bag. And he'd displayed it prominently on his lap all the way home, rewarded with a mixture of envious and admiring glances from anyone who looked like anyone.

Now he was ready to launch himself. He couldn't wait to see his mates' faces – trying to smile and saying, 'Great, mate,' while feeling sick to their stomachs. Gaz was still wearing last year's 501s, for God's sake. How pathetic was *that*?

Pete gave himself the twice-over. He was ready. Or was he? That little tuft of hair at the front just *wouldn't* spike. It kept breaking up, de-twisting like a piece of frayed rope. Back to the bathroom again. That gel – Zirth – cost a fortune. You'd expect the least it could do was produce a decent spike.

Pete's collection of brushes and creams and lotions stood in perfect military formation on the top shelf – a big notice in red magic marker screamed: DO NOT TOUCH. He knew the position of every pot, tube and bottle and could detect interference from a hundred paces. If his stupid little brother with his greasy hair and fat, baby face had been within a fingernail of any of them, he'd know.

Pete, Pete Ferris. Pete had been chewing over his name

for a few months now. Trying out a few tags. He'd finally managed to wean his mum off calling him 'Petey love' – in public, at least. There'd been a few times he could have killed her. He'd been considering a change. He was thinking about Jude, like that Jude guy in the movies. He was a cool dude, just like Pete, casual but sharp in the fashion stakes. Or even Dude. Dude Ferris sounded pretty neat to him, but he wasn't a hundred per cent sure . . . it could be naff in the wrong circles.

Now he really *was* ready. The rebellious spike glued into position, the fake tan giving him a gorgeous glow and setting off his streaked blond hair to perfection. Wow. If that little blonde, Milly, who he'd had his eye on for the past two weeks or so, didn't just fall into his lap, he would eat his Nikes.

Gareth (Gazza) and Si were hanging out in The Way Out, shooting sidelong glances at the door every time it swung open. They were itching with the need to be out and cruising.

Si, a tall, thin boy in black, with an earnest, questioning expression, looked at his watch. 'Let's give him ten minutes, eh? I'm sick of hanging around waiting for that guy. What's *up* with him, man?'

'You should know Pete by now,' said Gareth. 'Takes him half an hour to get his pants at the right angle, and that's just his boxers!'

They roared with laughter. Si with his hyena screech, Gaz with a deep-throated guffaw. They looked at each other, grinning. They were the lads, friends from way back, blood brothers out Saturday-nighting. Gazza sat back contentedly. He might not be the brightest beacon on the fashion scene but he certainly was king of the one-liners. He could shoot them faster than a premier-league striker in an empty goal.

'Pete's got something up his sleeve. Was full of himself on the phone. *Chirpy-chirpy, cheep-cheep.* I asked him, Hey, what's bubbling with you, man? And he goes, Nothing much. Hey, let's just say I got this feeling I'm gonna be sparking tonight.' Gaz did a fair impression of Pete with all the little hip-hop gyrations that had suddenly appeared in his body language over the past few weeks.

Si rolled his eyes. 'Sometimes, I think that guy is way out on a limb. I mean, where's he get the cash? That's what I wanna know. How does he afford all that gear?'

'You've seen the programme, haven't you – Bank of Mum and Dad?' said Gaz. 'Well, there you go – Bank of Divorced Dad's even better. And when you've got Bank of Guilty Divorced Dad With Big Cowboy Roofing Firm – you're laughing, man. Pete only has to snap his fingers and Bob's your Armani.'

At that exact moment, in walked the King of Cool.

'Hey, guys.'

It was even better than Pete expected. Gazza's jawline just about dropped to the floor when he eyeballed the new Ikos. Si, that long streak of water – Pete could see him squirming and thinking, How'd he *do it*?

'Hey, man – we said eight o'clock, not midnight. What's with you? This is the last time we're hanging around. OK?'

'Chill, chill. Who wants a drink, eh? Let's have one for the road.'

Of course, the boys weren't going to turn down a round, and anyway, Pete needed his fifteen minutes of fame. He needed them to take in every detail of his new gear, no distractions.

'Hey, cool jeans, man,' said Gazza. 'New?'

Pete wasn't the King of Cool for nothing. He looked down, surprised, as if the Ikos had suddenly oozed onto his legs like paint from a tube. 'What, these? Oh, yeah. Just got 'em, mate. Latest Ikos. Hit the streets today.'

Si was looking sick. He couldn't disguise it. Who could blame him? Look at those old black Levis that were practically pre-Ark, teamed with a none-too-clean T-shirt, and a leather jacket so last year it was turning retro already.

'Yeah, just nipped into town this morning – hot off the peg – what d'ya think? Cool, eh?'

Gazza rolled his eyes. Hey! Pete caught that Now that wasn't fair, was it? Just because he had the IQ to get ahead in the game. The big green eye, eh? Look at them, pathetic! They couldn't manage one compliment between them. Hadn't they *noticed* how deeply cool these jeans were, they were practically singing out loud. Hadn't they noticed the way they *fit* him, how lush they looked with his Armani T? 'Course they had. Sometimes he felt he was wasting his time with these dudes. He needed to be among the serious action.

He couldn't resist it. 'Hey, Gaz, heard from Emma lately?'

Emma, the love of Gaz's life, endless legs and jet-black hair down to her waist, had dumped him for a guy who worked in Mazos – the trendiest clothes shop in town. A real cool dude. He knew his Ikos from his Cavallis, that was for sure!

It did the trick. Gaz looked crestfallen, then he leant forward in his chair and looked daggers. 'As a matter of fact . . .'

The two boys looked expectantly. Pete was thinking, *Surely not . . .*

'As a matter *of fact* . . .'

'Well?'

'As a matter o-f f-a-c-t . . .'

Si was on the edge of his seat, and even Pete was paying close attention.

'As a matter *of fact* . . .'

'Well?'

Gaz fell back into his chair.

'No!'

Si snorted with laughter. Pete was incensed. How come that dude was able to turn everything around? Thought he was *so* funny. Pete just didn't get it.

They strode into the Electric like *The Good, the Bad and the Ugly* (an old but favourite film of Pete's with Clint Eastwood – the coolest dude in the universe) into the OK Saloon. That's what it felt like to Pete, anyway. He was Clint – of course – and Gaz and Si, well – it was a toss-up between them. Gaz and Si headed for the bar to get a round, and Pete stood poised at the top of the steps. Every eye in the place turned on him as he scanned the room like a hired gun, looking for his prey.

Milly Fairly, a bundle of cute blond, shimmering female, was over in the corner hanging out with her pals Rachel D and that dopey girl Babs, or Gabs or whatever she was called. Shame. He'd be forced to let her within his orbit –

with her fat stomach practically waterfalling over her too-tight supermarket jeans. But needs must, he thought. As soon as he and Milly were an item he'd forbid her to hang around with that dweeb. He would teach her a thing or two about style, about cool. She'd have to know how to cut it if she was going to be his girl. Hey, just the way his new Ikos were cutting it. This was *so* his night.

Back in his room that same night, in fact at two o'clock the following morning, Pete Ferris, the coolest dude in the universe, lay wide awake on his bed, contemplating his Calvins in deep confusion. *What had that been all about?* How *could* that have happened?

Score one to Pete. He'd got the girls over to their table. That was down to him, and two rounds. Score two to Pete. He'd got Milly up on the dancefloor, he'd got her synching with his moves. He was *sure* he was in. Every time he'd shimmied towards her, she'd shimmied backwards – forwards, backwards; forwards, backwards. That was cool synching.

Then, when they got back to the table, what did she do? She practically fell into Gazza's lap, screeching with laughter every time he opened his mouth. Something was badly wrong. Then Rachel D, who he supposed wasn't bad-looking in her way, and who (he was thinking) he could just about settle for – give Milly something to think about – started coming on to Si, that long streak of water. So there *he* was, the King of Cool, with moon-face dweeb, Gabs or Babs – Gags, as far as he was concerned – flashing her braces at him, lolling all over him, her stomach practically falling into his lap like a puppy dog. And every time he tried to inch away, she inched closer! He was frozen in mortification. Welded to the seat. Whatever he did was going to break his cool. He shot a dagger eye at Gaz. Gaz *knew* he fancied Milly. How could he do that? And how could she prefer Gaz to him? Gaz in his stupid 501s and Oxfam T.

Finally, he mumbled something, shoved off that Gabby dork and headed for the Men's. He didn't want to play any more. Oh, no! Let them get on with it. Milly was probably just trying to wind him up, trying to get the old green eye going. There couldn't be any other explanation.

He was on his way out when Gaz and Si came up and said they were off to Standards with the girls. Gaz smirked: 'Hey, Pete. Babs's really into you, lucky geezer!'

Pete let rip: 'What! That ugly little cow – I wouldn't give her left earlobe the time of day!'

There was a screech from behind, like a wounded parrot. He turned to see Babs, her face crumbling, and Milly striding forward: 'You *pig*! Who do you think *you* are? Ugly yourself! Bean-Face!'

Bean-Face!

BEAN-FACE!

What did *that* mean?

After a restless night, Pete stood in the bathroom, giving the mirror a little less than his usual full-on. He studied his chops from every angle. Bean-Face! True, his cheeks were a smidgen on the chubby side, but hey! That made him look cute, didn't it? For a second he felt a little knot of anxiety in his stomach; the mirror wasn't giving him its usual hundred per cent approval; in fact, it wasn't giving anything away, one way or the other. He pulled at his spikes and put on a mean expression, like Johnny D in *Pirates* about to slay his enemy in one lethal movement. Pah! She was talking rubbish, that Milly. Didn't know class when it jumped up and hit her in the face. Just some jealous little tart. He looked at the row of toiletries, standing to attention: his team! Suddenly, the little knot of anxiety dissolved like a lump of sugar. He gave the mirror another Johnny D. He was cool, he was mean. That Gazza! It was all his fault. He was Pete Ferris the Avenger. Pete the Unforgiver.

Gaz had called three times, and each time Pete's hand, as if on autopilot, shot to his shining new top-of-the-range Samsung with photo and video, but he stopped himself, just in time. Even though he was interested (OK he was *eaten up* with curiosity) as to how it had gone down with Milly and her mates, he was determined not to talk to *them* after that shameful performance. He was going it alone now. Traitors. Call themselves *friends*. No! He was cutting them out of his life, giving them the big elbow. For ever. Dweebs. Geeks. He didn't know why he had hung around with them in the first place. Gazza and Si – they'd always been jealous. Now he, Pete, was moving on.

So that was why, the following Saturday, having broken with tradition and bypassed The Way Out for the first time since he could remember, he was sitting in a swanky new bar called Wicked, aloof and alone. This was where the action was, where the cool dudes hung out. He sat by the window, surveying the scene and fighting a horrible feeling that rose up every time he thought of what Milly had said.

'Bean-Face.'

For the past few days those words had been eating away at his heart, his very soul. They sat in his stomach like an unwelcome guest, uninvited, but irrevocably *there*. He stared moodily over the top of his glass.

Hey man, who are *they*?

'Anyone sitting here?' In front of him stood the coolest people Pete had ever seen. Two guys and a girl. The girl had jet-black hair, so shiny you could practically see your face in it. Short red PVC skirt with zips up the side and fishnet tights. The boys were in recycled punk. But not overdone. They exuded style and confidence. And strength, in a funny way. No one'd mess with them.

'Na-ah. 's OK,' came out all high-pitched and strangled.

Stupid! Pete pretended to cough but only succeeded in spluttering his last gulp of Coke over the table. Keep cool! Keep cool!

The three dudes sat down at the end of the table and Pete strained to hear their conversation. They were talking about the town. Something about the people . . . the kind of people who lived here . . . a competition or something. His ears were tuned like radar on high alert.

Suddenly, one of the lads looked at him. 'Hi.' He smiled. 'You live here, mate?'

Pete nearly dropped his drink. Keep cool. Keep cool! 'Yeah.' This time his voice came out too low. What was the matter with him?

The lad continued, 'We're just passing through. We're here for a project, for college. Looking at different towns, different scenes.'

'What do you do?'

'We're designers.'

Designers! Pete knew his cool was in jeopardy. Calm down. Calm down. The girl looked at him and grinned. Gorgeous. His heart was racing.

'Well, talking of designers . . .' He couldn't help it. He tapped both knees.

'They the new Ikos?' said the other lad, more as a statement than a question.

'Hey, you really know your stuff, dudes,' said Pete, beaming, beginning to relax. He rubbed his chest. Hopefully they would notice his T was Armani.

The chat went on. Pete was on form – there was nothing he didn't know about designer gear. He was the ace, the frontman. The three strangers seemed riveted, hanging on to his every word. He had *the power*. Gaz and Si could go to hell. He felt embarrassed that he'd ever hung out with them. These designer dudes, they were ice cool, man. They had a look, unique. Pete was itching to ask where they got their gear. Probably designed it themselves.

The girl shifted in her seat and picked something up from the floor. Pete's eyes sparked. Bags. Lush bags, black and silver; ice blue . . .

'What ya got there, then?'

'Oh, these? Just some new gear we're researching. Really cool stuff.'

'Yeah?'

'Yeah. This stuff, it's pretty new. We're looking for people – hip guys – to try it out. Get some feedback. It's so hot, it's not even hit the scene yet.' She looked at him, straight, with her minxy green eyes, as if she was passing on a state secret.

This was *it*. Pete's whole body was crying out for those bags. Aching for them. He was daring to think . . . hip guys. Is that why they parked themselves with me, after eyeballing my gear?

'Coo-oool. Gi's a look, then.'

The girl opened one of the bags and pulled out a flat tissue-wrapped package. She carefully opened it up. A black T, shot across the front with a silver blade-like logo. Cap sleeves. Cool as ice.

'Lush!' said Pete.

'Like it?' She picked up another bag. The ice-blue one. More tissue. This was class. She pulled out a pair of trousers. She held them up. Silver-grey, scooped at the ankle.

'Man!' said one of the lads. 'Those are so . . . *tomorrow* . . .'

Pete was salivating. Will they . . .

The girl was looking at him again, in that way. If only Gaz and Si could see him now.

'Hey,' she said. 'I just thought . . . I don't suppose you'd want to take part in this project – try out this gear? Get the feel. Give us the feedback. You're just the kind of guy we're looking for. And looks like you're the right size, too.'

Yay! It was going down. Just as he'd hoped. Those bags were as good as in his hands.

One of the lads, the one in retro leather and Sixties ankle boots, explained the deal. They were holding a review at the uni, next Saturday, getting all the cool dudes together. They were filming it for the final-year show. 'You'd have to come, along,' he said. 'In the gear.'

Pete was practically hyperventilating. Keep cool. Keep cool. He called Johnny D into play, the old narrow eye.

Bean-Face was gone for ever. *This* was who he was; the top man, mixing with the real thing – these designer dudes – they knew class when they saw it.

The girl handed him a flyer. 'Hey, don't spread this around, will you? This is an *exclusive* scene – know what I mean?' She smiled at him, full on, flicking her curtain of hair over her shoulder. He almost fainted with joy. 'I'm Isa, by the way. And this is Rob and James T. What's your name?'

'Jude . . . Jude Ferris.'

Well, he couldn't resist it, could he? He was on his mobile like greased lightning on full throttle, gabbing with Gaz and then Si as if nothing had happened.

'Where ya bin, mate?' 'Just chilling.' 'Must've rung you a hundred times.' 'Hey what you doin' next Saturday? I've got a cool gig fixed up. Wanna come?' He gave just enough away to get them hooked. 'Meet up, yeah? Uni. Three o'clock.'

What did he care now, about that tarty little Milly? Gaz was welcome to her. She was *no one*! But that Isa. My God! She was definitely giving him the eye. He couldn't wait to see their faces when the coolest chick in the universe started up with him. Of course, he'd have to lose them when he got inside. He didn't want his new mates clocking their naff hair and gear. But they'd see all right. They'd be green, especially Gaz. Isa with her jet-black hair was like Emma with knobs on. He'd be sick; so green he'd be sprouting leaves.

Saturday. Pete, with Gaz and Si in tow, stood in a small crowd outside the uni waiting for the doors to open. Gaz and Si, trying to look as if they couldn't care less. Gaz looking round the gathering crowd with that 'so what' look on his face. Si, looking at his watch like he had something better to do. As if! Pete knew the truth. They were gagging with curiosity.

And Pete was feeling good. A1, Ace, King, Johnny D cool. His hair was a masterwork – every spike lovingly hand-crafted, and standing up in perfect formation. His new gear, the T especially – with its sharp cap sleeves gliding over his tanned biceps – was to die for – he couldn't wait for the gorgeous Isa to clock how drop-dead he looked.

Weird, though. Some of the dudes waiting with them didn't look so hot. In fact, the man in front of him looked positively Dweebsville. Must be some helper or something, Pete told himself. Gaz was also squinting at the crowd, 'Hey, Pete, mate – what did you say this gig was . . .'

'Well, as I *told you* . . . I met these three . . .'

Gaz and Si were not listening . . . Gaz's head was all stalked up, like a periscope, eyeballing the crowd. 'Hey, man, have you seen . . .'

There was an annoying scuffling noise. He'd been vaguely aware of some whinging, neck-ache kid behind him. And he'd been thinking, shouldn't let kids in here, man. How uncool is that.

Pete turned. It was a small boy, not more than eight or nine, holding on to his mother's hand, and he was pointing at Pete.

Why was he pointing at him?

'That man's got my jumper!'

*

Pete just had time to clock the silver-dagger T — same as his — but teamed with cheap jeans, scuffed supermarket trainers, when the doors opened.

A huge poster, four metres high — neon bright, cheap — screamed out from the foyer:

THE LATTERLANE CHALLENGE!

can YOU tell the difference?

in association with St Mark's College of Art
Year Three Design Department

First there was nothing but silence, a buzzing silence in his ears. Pete just couldn't take it in. Couldn't get from where he'd been two minutes ago to where he was now. Suddenly, Gaz's deep-throated guffaw, Si's high-pitched screeching burst into his brain like a herd of demented hyenas, and the true horror hit home. Latterlane! That cheap supermarket so-called 'brand'. The butt of a million jokes. That's what his cool gear was! He was dressed from top to toe in *Latterlane*. And then, as if it couldn't get much worse, he saw, near the end of the line, that Gabby dweeb with some old woman, probably her mother, in a manky old fleece and *leggings*. He felt as if he was going into spasm, the odious gear crawling on his body like some filthy slime.

Gaz and Si were killing themselves, doubled up. Gaz was grasping his stomach; he could hardly breathe.

'Hey, man, real cool—' he snorted '—*real* cool. Can *you* tell the difference? Looks like you can't then, mate. So we may as well get off home now, eh?'

Pete sat on the bus. His world had crashed around him. He was Pete again, a hundred per cent. A hundred per cent Bean-Face. The sickening clothes sat on his body like a curse. He couldn't wait to get home and rip them to shreds. Every speck, every smidgen of cred he'd had in this town was gone. Those creeps! How could he have fallen for it? He'd been set up, like a brainless duck on a shooting range just to prove some point for their pathetic art school *project*. And Gaz and Si'd tell everyone, that was for sure. Gaz's 'oh, I'm so funny' patter was already echoing in his ears. He'd tell Milly, that was the worst. Just thinking about it made Pete squirm. He didn't think she was a tart, really. He had *truly* liked her, *deep down*. Some sad loser looked at him through the window; it was a moment before he realised it was his own reflection. He slumped in his seat, everything gone but his core; he was bone without flesh, raw meat.

A few stops before home, lost in anger and self-loathing, he suddenly noticed a girl sitting opposite him. She must have just got on and he was so eaten up with misery that he hadn't even noticed. She was real cool – pretty, with pale, golden hair and a sweet, open face. Normally he'd be making some moves. Now, he stayed slumped, unable to move. No point in even trying to cover up this loathsome gear. She probably thought he was some pathetic loser on the way home from a second-rate supermarket sale.

Bean-Face.

It took a few moments for him to realise the girl was

smiling at someone. Some lucky bloke was getting some action. He shifted in his seat, sticky and uncomfortable. Outside the window, the sky had turned dark, as if it was going to rain, and he suddenly felt like crying. He glanced up. She *seemed* to be looking at him, but he wasn't falling for that again. Oh no! He'd been fooled once and that was once too often. She smiled again. Pete looked up and down.

There was no one next to him.

There was no one else on the bus.

His mind spun. She *is* looking at me, she's looking at *me*.

This story was inspired by 'The Emperor's New Clothes'. CC

Taking Flight

Eloise Swann's mother died when Eloise was only three years old. Eloise could scarcely remember her. Her threadbare memories matched the familiar photos so exactly that Eloise doubted they were real memories at all, just well-worn stories that fitted the pictures. As a small girl, she had loved to sit on a little stool, turning the pages of the photo album and chatting to the people who inhabited them; they took on a life within her imagination that was easily confused with memory.

Eloise's father was hardly more real to her than her dead mother. His job as a government adviser took him all over the world and he became distant from his children, touching down on their lives from time to time but never staying around long enough to understand them. So it was fortunate that Eloise had three doting older brothers who had been brought up by a loving mother. A succession of nannies kept the family on the rails, never starving the children of the warmth and affection they needed to flourish, nor loving them so much that their inevitable departure was too painful a wrench.

As they grew older the boys were sent off, one by one, to boarding school in Scotland. It was a cold and comfortless institution, dedicated to shaping leaders of men, and Eloise's brothers loathed it. Each time they came home for the holidays they were unhappier than the time before, and they grew wild and unruly. The nannies moved on more quickly. But however many small items the brothers stole from the shops or fires they lit in letterboxes or washing lines they peppered with BB guns, they adored their pretty little sister. They loved her for herself and they loved her for their lost mother.

Not only did Eloise resemble her mother physically, but, like her, she surrounded herself with colourful fabrics: bright silks for dolls' clothes, dyed wool for knitting and weaving, outrageous patchwork on her jeans. She made leaf collages and collected feathers and shells and stones.

Eloise missed her brothers dreadfully when they were away, especially Patrick, the youngest and closest to her.

When Eloise was thirteen years old, the supply of nannies dried up. The children were now old enough to look after themselves during their father's prolonged absences, but what finally sent the last nanny scurrying was the arrival of Deirdre. Deirdre had been Mr Swann's PA for years and had longed, ever since the death of the first Mrs Swann, to become the second. She had never met his children and had never wanted to.

Now, mistress of Mr Swann's house at last, but faced with a sulky Eloise and three wild teenage boys, Deirdre wanted the place to herself. It was high time Eloise also went to boarding school. Mr Swann decided that Eloise should go to her mother's school, a progressive co-educational establishment near the sea. He wanted her to be happy, to remain surrounded by colour and light and warmth. The school agreed to take her in the spring term. He drove Eloise there himself on the first day and kissed her tenderly goodbye.

But however free and easy the new school, Eloise was desperately unhappy and lonely. She missed her home and her old schoolfriends. Her fellow pupils were all so confident and self-assured. They slouched around in torn jeans, raggedy jumpers, big jewellery. They knew what music was cool. They talked about sex and drugs in a knowing way and swore a lot. For their part they were suspicious of Eloise's prettiness – the girls envious, the boys unnerved. The headmaster's romantic and good-looking son Leo fell in love with her instantly, but he kept quiet about it, for the time being at least.

Eloise found solace in e-mail and the craft workshop. Fay Morgan, the elderly craft teacher, presided over the barn-like building and kept the doors open and the wood stove burning most of the time for pupils such as Eloise. Fay quickly recognised Eloise's feeling for textiles and colours and enjoyed showing her how to spin and weave from hemp and flax and other ancient yarns that were making their way back into fashion.

At weekends, when most of the boarders returned home, Eloise stayed in the workshop. On Sunday afternoons, the remaining pupils were encouraged to go for walks, and Eloise took pleasure in blowing along the beach and watching the colours in the sea or picking up the round stones and keeping them for comfort in her pockets, marvelling at their smoothness. On the beach, with no one for company but the squealing sea birds, Eloise could imagine that her brothers were with her, racing along the sand, the wind in their hair.

Eloise quickly became a favourite of Fay Morgan, who had a project in mind for her. 'Nettles!' said Fay to Eloise. 'I want you to make fabric from them.'

'I know you can make soup from them,' said Eloise, 'and dye. Mum had some wool samples dyed with nettles. Onions, too. She'd labelled them all.'

'It's the fibres,' said Fay. 'They make yarn. Napoleon's army was dressed in cloth made from nettles.'

'Cool!' said Eloise. 'I'd love to make clothes from nettles. It would be like creating something from nothing. Like making it up as you go along.' The project fired Eloise's imagination. She spent hours on the Internet trying to find out just how to create thread from nettles. She doodled during her other lessons and designed a boy's shirt and jacket, and a skirt for herself. It kept her occupied and happy in a way that she had not been for a long time. She and Fay planned to include the finished clothes in the art display on open day.

The weeks ground on through January and February. It was cold and bleak and bare – not even nettle shoots showed green above the earth. But March came in, windy and warm, and Eloise saw that soon there would be enough new nettles to pick.

The next Sunday she set off to the beach with a basket in case she found a good crop on her way. Leo spotted her from his bedroom window, enchanted by the beautiful girl with her basket, her long fair hair blowing in the wind, and decided to follow her.

Eloise did indeed find a fine stand of nettles and, remembering about 'grasping the nettle', tried to pick them without gloves, but was badly stung for her pains. She put them in her basket and hurried down to the sea, hoping to bathe the stings in saltwater. Three magnificent white swans were bobbing about on the tide near her usual stretch of sand. Eloise held back to watch them; she was a little afraid of swans. She sat down on a rock and stroked three white feathers that had washed up, allowing the sound of the wild wind and the waves to soothe her, wishing as always that her brothers could be there with her.

Suddenly, a Land Rover came bumping across the sand towards her, loud music pouring from its windows. Eloise jumped to her feet in alarm, but it skidded to a halt in a flurry of sand and a boy leapt out and came running towards her. 'Eloise! It's us! We've come to take you away!' It was Oliver, her middle brother. John, the oldest, was at the wheel, and Patrick was in the back. They were all grinning.

Eloise could not believe her eyes. She stood stock-still in surprise, wondering that her wish had really come true. She shook her head and tried to speak in a normal voice. 'Where did you get the car?' was all she could think to ask at first. 'I didn't know you could drive, John!'

'It doesn't matter where we got it,' said Olly. 'Aren't you pleased to see us? Aren't you amazed we managed to find you?'

'Of course I am,' said Eloise. 'It's wonderful! I can't quite believe you're here. Did you drive all the way from Scotland today?'

'Yup,' said John. 'It took seven hours.'

'We're *free!*' yodelled Patrick. 'Get in, little sister! Bring your basket of green thingies, you magpie, you.'

Eloise climbed in after them and they roared away on to the road, watched from the far end of the beach by a bemused Leo. Had he just seen Eloise being kidnapped? He feared for her and walked back to the school wondering whether he should mention what he'd witnessed to his father.

As they drove, the March afternoon grew darker and wilder. 'Where are we going?' asked Eloise. It was brilliant being with her brothers, but it was noisy both inside and outside the Land Rover, and John's driving was erratic.

'Wherever you want!' said Olly. 'So long as it's not Scotland, home, or your school.'

'Let's go and have tea somewhere,' said Eloise. 'I'm hungry, and I can't hear myself think, let alone talk, with this racket.'

'Your wish is our command,' said John, and parked on double yellow lines outside a little teashop. The three boys all had to stoop to go in the door, their voices loud in the genteel atmosphere.

'Have you got any money?' Eloise asked.

'We've got a credit card,' said Olly, giggling and tapping his nose.

John called the middle-aged waitress over. 'Four of your best cream teas, please,' he said, tipping back in the spindly chair until the legs were at risk of snapping.

'John!' said Eloise. 'Careful – you'll break it!'

'I think that would be the least of our crimes,' said Olly, still giggling.

Eloise looked at her three darling brothers. They were all giggling. 'Are you OK?' she asked anxiously. 'You're not–? Are you off your heads?'

'Might be,' said Olly. 'A little bit. And what if we are?'

'But John – you're *driving*!'

'I'm OK,' said John. 'Don't worry about me.'

'I'm worrying about *me*!' said Eloise, as their cream teas appeared with much tinkling of cutlery and china and straightening of the tablecloth, which made Olly giggle even more. 'I don't want to be driven by someone who's–' She shut her mouth as the disapproving waitress flapped around her. 'Are you all *mad*?' she finished in a stage whisper.

The boys looked crestfallen. 'We wanted to liberate you,' they said, 'from the dreadful Deirdre. And ourselves, too, from the fascists who run our school.'

'My school isn't run by fascists,' said Eloise. 'Actually, I get on really well with this teacher called Fay. She teaches textiles.'

'Like Mum, you mean?' said John, sober again.

'I suppose so,' said Eloise. 'I never thought of that. But that's what those nettles are for. I'm going to make cloth from them.'

'And you think *we're* mad!' guffawed Olly.

'Look,' said Eloise, suddenly nervous and afraid of what all this madness could lead to. 'I want you to take me back to school. And I want you to go back to Scotland. I'm not going to ask about the Land Rover or the stupid credit card, but I think you're out of your minds. You don't want to get expelled! Anything's better than being at home with Deirdre. You'll be out of there next year, John. You can go travelling all you want.'

The boys sat over their tea like naughty children. 'Just keep a low profile. That's what I'm doing,' said Eloise. 'I just get through it. I figure that if I work away at this nettle project, that will bring me a year closer to doing whatever I want, maybe to living with you lot again – without Deirdre. To us all being free.'

She paid for the tea from her own purse.

It was quite dark when they drew up outside Eloise's school. 'You could be back in Scotland before it gets light and anyone notices the Land Rover is missing,' she said, tearfully kissing them goodbye.

Patrick, the youngest brother, was crying too. He hugged Eloise. 'I miss you, little sis,' he said, his salty tears spilling onto her stung hands as she cupped his face. 'I hate my school. I don't want to go back there. They treat us like we're in the army already. At least you're somewhere that's human.'

'Go back for now,' said Eloise. 'Maybe we can talk Dad round to moving you. But go back – or they'll send you somewhere worse. I don't know what Deirdre will make Dad do with you all if you're caught. Go back, please. I won't say a word to anyone.'

Patrick climbed back in the Land Rover with the others. None of them was giggling now. Eloise picked up her basket and blew them a kiss. 'Drive safely!' she called quietly after them.

Leo watched it all from the shadows. He didn't know they were her brothers. Jealousy of the boy whose face she'd held so tenderly stabbed at his heart. But Eloise was safely back at school so he decided to keep what he'd seen to himself. He didn't want to get her into trouble.

Leo contrived to sit by Eloise at supper and coaxed her into conversation. He wanted to hear her side of the story. Eloise managed to say very little in response to Leo's jokes and questions but she started to like him.

The next day Fay found some stout gloves and a useful knife for Eloise so that she could cut long nettles without hurting herself again. Eloise went out with her basket in the evening before the light faded completely and headed for the stand near the beach. It was some distance from the school, but she needed time and space to reflect on what had happened the day before. She was tempted to ring her brothers to make sure they'd got back safely, but thought better of it. She could e-mail them later.

Eloise filled her basket with nettles and turned for home. Suddenly there was a commotion amongst the trees; branches shaking and leaves rustling. She hurried on, scared. 'Eloise!' called a male voice. 'Eloise! Over here!'

It was Olly. 'Why are you still here?' said Eloise, appalled. 'I thought you'd gone back!'

'We can't.' Patrick appeared at Olly's side. His eyes were wide and frightened. 'We've stolen a car, Eloise, and a credit card. They'll do us. And it won't just be antisocial behaviour. John could go down for this.'

'You've got to keep quiet, Eloise,' John spoke from the Land Rover which Eloise made out for the first time hidden amongst the bushes.

'Got any food on you?' wheedled Olly. 'We're starving.'

'Oh, honestly!' Eloise was torn between pity and anger.

'We have to stay in hiding,' said Patrick. 'Deirdre would happily see us in boot camp. And you know what happens to people there.'

'I can't help you tonight,' said Eloise. 'Do you want me to get into trouble too? Spear a fish or something. I'll come down tomorrow night for some more nettles and bring you something to eat. Now I've got to get back!' She stumbled back to school in the darkness, cursing her brothers for being such idiots.

Each evening after that, Eloise slipped away in the twilight with food in her basket for her brothers and returned with it filled with nettles. Each time she was terrified of being seen, terrified of being followed, even though it was still bliss to see her brothers every day. Sometimes Leo spotted her returning. He knew she had a secret.

Five days later John, Olly and Patrick suddenly disappeared. Eloise had no idea where they had gone. They didn't answer their phones and though she sent them desperate e-mails there was no reply there either. She had no one to talk to. She couldn't tell anyone the boys had been here so recently. Because, inevitably, the missing brothers made the headlines.

The headmaster felt certain that Eloise must know something about her brothers' whereabouts, and called her in again and again to try and extract the truth from her. But Eloise would say nothing – she knew nothing – and each time he grew more frustrated with her. Deirdre was summoned to the school and threatened to take her unco-operative stepdaughter home then and there, but Fay Morgan intervened and said that it would do Eloise no good, far better for her to stay at school where her project would take the poor girl's mind off the fate of the boys. Why wouldn't they believe she was telling the truth when she said she didn't know where they were?

Police came to the school. The place was crawling with them and Eloise half hoped they would find the boys and the Land Rover still hidden in the woods, but they never did. She prayed that they would get in touch when they could.

In the safe haven that was the workshop, Eloise laid the nettles out to dry before soaking them and found that if she trampled them they turned into a mass of fibres. The trampling released the formic acid in the nettles and brought tears to her eyes, but the day they managed to twist the fibres into yarn Eloise and Fay hugged one another and danced about. This was truly something from nothing!

One Sunday afternoon Eloise walked to the beach as she used to before the boys went into hiding. She was more lonely than ever. Only the swans bobbing on the tide reminded her of the time her brothers had been there with her. As she turned for home Leo suddenly appeared on the path ahead of her. He looked determined, as if he had made his mind up about something. Eloise felt alarmed by the expression on his face. In fact, Leo had been specifically asked by his father to question Eloise about her missing brothers. But Leo could keep a secret. He had told no one about what he'd witnessed before. The happy realisation that it was only her brother he'd seen Eloise kissing blotted out the need to tell the truth to his father or the police. All he planned to do now was simply to kiss her himself, and he was very determined about that.

He saw Eloise walking with her basket, her cheeks pink from the wind off the sea. She looked up at him, nervous as a fawn. Since her interviews with the headmaster she'd found it harder to relax with his son. But here they were together, with the woodland path ahead and the sea behind, and he seemed tall and comforting and gorgeous to a girl who was lonely and starting to fall in love with him.

Leo didn't need to say anything. He held out his arms, almost helplessly, and Eloise ran into them. They clung together tightly, her head against his chest, Leo's face buried in the sea-scented silkiness of her hair, before he sought out her lips with his and they kissed.

They spent the rest of the spring afternoon on the beach together, watching the swans and kissing some more. Words weren't necessary.

So Eloise had a boyfriend. The kissing was great, but the talking was harder. 'What's the rest of your family like?'

'My mother died when I was three. I don't really want to talk about my family. I can't tell you anything about my brothers, you know I can't.'

'Why don't you go home at weekends? Why do your parents never come and visit you? Where do you live?'

'I just don't want to talk about anything to do with home, OK?'

'You're so pretty. I can't believe you haven't had loads of other boyfriends.'

'I don't want to talk about boys. None apart from you, that is. What's it like always living at school? What's it like having a headmaster for a dad?'

'OK. Let's talk music and books and films.'

'Fine by me.'

'Have you read *Catcher in the Rye*?'

'Kiss me.'

The missing boys were national news. No one knew where they were. Everyone knew about the stolen Land Rover and the credit card and the string of minor crimes that preceded the larger one. They knew their father was out of his mind with worry but that their glamorous stepmother was convinced they were a bad lot. Everyone knew they had a sister. Everyone knew the sister was Eloise and that she was saying nothing, a fact which made her somehow guilty, even though she protested that she *knew* nothing. It gave her mild celebrity status, but no comfort about the missing brothers.

Eloise continued to send e-mails to them, hurriedly deleting them as soon as they were sent and receiving no replies. Fay helped her try to live a normal life as the search went on. Before long, Eloise had enough nettle yarn to start weaving cloth. Fay threaded up a second loom and the two of them wove in companionable silence. Soon they had several metres of cloth. It was cream-coloured, fine, and silky. All that remained was for them to dye it and make it into clothes. Eloise cut out her skirt, a shirt and jacket that she imagined for John and Olly, and there was still enough cloth left over to make something eccentric for Patrick. It comforted her to picture them in the clothes she was making.

The nettle project took up all Eloise's spare time. Leo was interested but only up to a point, and he began to resent the way it kept Eloise away from him. He retaliated by trying to make her talk on the subject she found most difficult. He was in a tough situation. The police were convinced that the boys' sister had information that would lead to them. Leo wanted only to protect Eloise. He never told her that he knew her secret.

'A skirt for you, and *three* tops for boys you're making, did you say?' he asked now, beginning to think maybe she deserved to be trapped. But then she looked so flustered that he let it go. But *why* wouldn't she just speak and incriminate her brothers? He would lose her if she didn't, he had no doubt.

Finally, frustrated by her endless silence, he shouted at her, '*Please*, Eloise! Eloise, I *saw* you that day. I *saw* you on the beach with three boys and a Land Rover. I *know* they were here!' Eloise looked at him open-mouthed with fear and her blue eyes filled with tears.

'Have – have you told anyone?'

'*No!*' he retorted. 'I didn't want to hurt *you*. But please, please just say your brothers came here in the stolen car. And say where they are. Please. I don't want to lose you just because your brothers won't own up.'

'I don't know where they are,' said Eloise sullenly, and clamped her mouth shut as the tears ran down her face. She would say no more and Leo left her with a heavy heart.

*

It was open day. The other textile students were mounting a fashion show with a catwalk and music and dry ice. But without the real models for her garments, Eloise lost heart and pinned them out flat and two-dimensional alongside photos and text about how they had been conceived and fashioned. Fay had begged her to let some of the other students model her clothes and show them off, but Eloise was adamant that they would only look good on the people they'd been made for, and she didn't want to model her skirt on her own.

Leo was playing in a football match all morning, but he and Eloise were barely speaking to each other these days. He told her that she couldn't love him if she didn't trust him with her secrets. Her silence might be protecting her brothers but now it was incriminating her – and didn't she see how stupid that was?

Eloise sat on the lawn under the blossom trees near the car park, plucking at the grass and watching the other children meeting up with their parents. It made her feel left out all over again. She'd e-mailed her father and her brothers (not Deirdre) about the show, but as usual, no one had replied. What was going to become of them all? She felt sure the boys were OK, not dead or anything, but they'd have to come out of hiding one day, and what fate lay in store for them then? And she had aided and abetted them, hadn't she? She'd withheld information, perverted the course of justice. She'd be in the sort of trouble Deirdre would relish, too.

A taxi pulled up so close to Eloise that she moved back hastily. Three boys climbed out. Eloise saw them before they saw her. It was like a dream, a vision. 'John! Olly! Oh, Patrick!' She threw herself at her beloved brothers.

'Decided to come,' said John. 'Took the train.'

'Need the toilet,' said Olly.

'This place looks even better in daylight,' said Patrick.

'Come with me!' said Eloise. 'I've got a job for you!'
There would be time later to discover the truth.

Eloise strode down the catwalk with the three handsome boys in their nettle garments and it was suddenly crystal clear to the world that these were her three lost brothers and that soon the truth would be out. Meanwhile Patrick won everyone's hearts in his asymmetric top.

Afterwards Leo came up and hugged her and she introduced him to John, Olly and Patrick. 'We decided to hand ourselves in,' John told him. 'We've been in a squat in London and it was getting pretty rancid. People were threatening to turn us in and we didn't want to give them the pleasure. And I don't want to give our stepmother an opportunity to upset my sister any more. I'm taking the blame. I'll have to do community service but at least I've left school now. Olly's punishment is having to stay there for another two years. But Olly's quite thick-skinned. He'll cope.' He nodded in Patrick's direction. 'I want to persuade Dad to send my little brother here. What do you think, Leo? Would your father take him on?'

John looked over to Eloise for approval but she was gazing, distracted, into the sky. Four beautiful swans were flying overhead, the beating of their wings strong and bold, like the beating of four hearts.

This story was inspired by 'The Wild Swans'. KP

Princess

My name is Daniel Banks. Who am I? Well, I hardly know myself.

Son, student, musician, best mate. Prat.

Prat. Yes. That is absolutely what I felt like when I got up to play at the school concert on Friday. Daniel Prat.

But not for long.

I'd been on edge all day – know why? I was about to play a set of three songs I'd *written myself* to the whole school. Alone and unaccompanied.

I was terrified.

And Alex – idiot, best mate, blagger – had gone on and on: 'Don't close your eyes, man. Look at the audience!

Look into my eyes, Danny Boy, and tell me you're listening. *Don't sing with your eyes closed.*' I knew. I knew that was a big no-no. All the books say it. Look at the audience, engage them. Don't, whatever you do, close your eyes. Well, not only do I close my eyes, but according to Alex, I keep my head down as well. So this time, I was determined to look up and out, eyes wide open in a sort of 'Look at me, I'm a superstar' sort of way. And what did I do?

I closed my eyes and put my head down.

But . . .

Big but . . .

. . . after a few blurry, wobbly seconds of agony I realised something. There was silence. No laughing, no heckling. My songs, precious to me but potentially hilarious to the world outside my head, potentially *ridiculous*, were being listened to. And the more I got going the more I got into it. They sort of took on a life of their own and I was thinking, these songs are good, man. They are *living*.

When I finished I couldn't help smiling. A few seconds' silence and then applause. Not just clapping, but some cheering too (probably Alex, I thought, but knowing really there were others too). I even stood up and bowed. Rather pathetic, I know, but there was a lot of noise and I felt the performance needed a full stop somehow. When I came off the stage and walked down the aisle, I felt a buzz – like a ripple of something. Girls. A ripple of girls. That's the only way I can put it. I felt them looking at me. Eyes wide open.

Then afterwards, at the party: Rachel Downey! The fittest girl in school. Black hair, white smile a mile wide. Great legs. She was all over me. I couldn't believe it. 'That was great, Dan,' she said, actually *touching me.*

I'd have fallen in love with her on the spot, even though I knew she had a boyfriend.

If I hadn't been in love already.

And so far gone that not even an army of Rachels could break through.

I was in love. It was my big secret. And had been since I was fourteen years old.

It happened like this: I was mooning around town – the music shop to be exact – lusting after this beautiful Gibson guitar that I could never, ever afford. The summer fair was on but I wasn't that interested, except they sometimes had a few second-hand music stalls where you could pick up some interesting stuff for next to nothing – old soul or R&B, which was what I was into at the time. So I wandered over and was flicking through a box of scratched CDs when a band started up. I wasn't bothered; I'd been to these things before and they usually had some fourth-rate local outfit churning out covers of old hits. Not my scene.

But this time, something happened. Just as I was thinking I'd had enough, I heard this voice. It seemed to pierce through the crowd, right into the space where I was standing. Silky, pure, with a little gravelly edge that went right through me. I made my way to the stage, pulled like fish on a line.

And there she was. Cassie Tyler. Although I didn't know that then.

Small, slim, long blond hair. But it wasn't just that – in fact, that was the bonus. As she sang she seemed to be looking up at something, rapt, her whole body poised, her arms lifted as if she was about to fly. And that voice, so sweet and full. It seemed miraculous that such a big voice could come out of someone so small! She sang a few covers of recent hits, and a couple of the band's own songs. I stood there, mesmerised. Then, I could hardly believe it, the band started the first few chords of an old Smokey Robinson song, 'The Tracks of My Tears', a song I had first heard on an old vinyl of Mum's. A song I *loved*. Wow. I got this melting feeling through my body; my chest seemed to cave in, as if I'd been punched by angels. I had to stop myself leaping onto the stage and sweeping her up in my arms. I could have done it! Prat.

I stayed for the whole set, right up front, and whooped and whistled with the rest of the crowd when they finished, to try to get them back on for an encore. More! More! I was hoarse with shouting. I needed to hear the name of the band, or better still, *her* name. But the compere didn't say it. He just said, 'Well, well . . . I think we all enjoyed that, didn't we? How about another round of applause?' I was desperate. Then I thought, never mind, I'll get it from the local paper, or the Internet.

I fought my way home through the crowds. I couldn't hear anything except an annoying buzz, like a radio not quite tuned in. And 'The Tracks of My Tears' round and round in my head. I was on another planet.

Wow!

I fell on my bed and just lay there in a heap, not knowing what to do. I felt as if I'd been hit by something, a rocket, a *meteorite*, that had sent me hurtling into another universe.

She was *gorgeous*!

Everything seemed different. Sort of sparkling. My computer by the window, now it held the answers, seemed to glow like some mystic, techno crystal ball. The sky seemed ultra blue, the clouds smooth as silk.

'Calm down, Danny Boy,' I told myself. 'First things first.'

It had taken about two seconds. Good old Google. Jewel. *Jew-el.* There was a blurry picture of the band on stage somewhere, but she was making that little movement with her hands – you could still see how lovely she was. Jewel! It seemed so right, because that's what she was like, something shining and precious. They were a local band, just starting out playing pubs and clubs. The blurb said:

Lead singer, Cassie Tyler, only sixteen years old, is already causing a stir on the local circuit with her powerful, soulful voice. It won't be long before she's snapped up by some enterprising recording company.

Cassie. That seemed right too. Sweet. And then something else miraculous happened.

I sat down and wrote my first complete song.

How many times had I tried to write a song? I could have started a recycling plant with the amount of paper I'd screwed up and thrown away. But now the words just fell into my head, the chords into my fingers, perfectly formed. *'A voice in the crowd / I knew it was you.'*

Mum had to call me three times for tea. I danced down the stairs, I couldn't help myself. I was buzzing.

She looked at me as if she'd seen a ghost. 'Daniel, what's up? You look like you've won the lottery or something.'

I smiled at her. She nearly dropped dead from the shock.

'I'm just in a good mood, Ma, OK?' I threw the ketchup up in the air and caught it with one hand without even looking. I'd never done that before!

She was still looking gobsmacked.

'That's all, Ma. Can't I just be *in a good mood*, eh?'

She looked quizzical. 'It's a girl, isn't it?' she ventured. 'That's what it is!'

I got stuck into my chips. 'None of your business.'

Alex. Alex. Alex. Why can't he just be straightforward? Normal. But then I suppose he wouldn't be Alex and he wouldn't make me laugh so much. Laugh until I could explode.

His room was crammed with every gizmo known to man, plus crisp wrappers, half-eaten biscuits, Coke cans by the dozen. I squeezed myself into a little island on the bed.

So, there in Alex's waste disposal unit, I offered up my first song. My hands were shaking. Nerves. You never knew which way Alex would go. He could be sharp, sarcastic – even when he liked something. Or he could be thoughtful and straightforward. This was so important to me. Important that Alex liked the song, truthfully. That he didn't muck about.

Sometimes, you know when something is good – or rather *feel* it and I didn't want to blow it by falling to pieces. But I lost my nerve as I went on and finished with those three chords that had come out of nowhere – a sort of descant cymbal sound that ricocheted around the room.

Complete silence.

'Well?'

'You are rubbish, man!' he said. 'How many times have I told you – *don't close your eyes!*'

'But what do you think?'

'What did I say? Rubbish!' But he was grinning. He ran his fingers through his hair – white-boy dreadlocks, stringy and flat, like some ropy old floor mop past its use-by date.

Still, in spite of the grin, I wasn't sure. I needed to know. I needed to hear it.

'Come on, mate, what do you think, *really* – given it's the first thing I've written myself.'

Alex being Alex couldn't say anything straight out. He shuffled about, keeping me waiting. His idea of fun. I think I hated him then. Eventually he looked at me and said, 'Can I be your manager, man?'

It's weird, being in love with someone you don't even know. But when she broke into that old Smokey song I just about melted on the spot. Love. It's a chemical thing, they say. I knew she was way out of my league, I wasn't even *in* a league then! Hadn't even had a proper girlfriend. But something had happened to me. I felt a *connection*! It was the music.

I began to write. To write and write and write. I was up in my room day and night, lyrics just falling onto the page. Mum was going crazy. You see, she wanted me studying. She wanted me to be – don't laugh – a concert pianist. She reckoned I'd get a scholarship to Parnell's – that big, swanky music school. Trouble was, and this was big trouble, I *didn't want* to be a concert pianist. I preferred the guitar, always had. I was sick to death of piano lessons. So she was mad because I was supposed to be practising Handel and Bach and all that stuff when all I wanted to do was write songs for Cassie, my golden girl.

I found out everything about her, which wasn't much more than I knew already: that she lived in Willminster, on the other side of town, that she had been to boarding school (which was obviously why I'd never clocked her before), that she was a gorgeous, talented, beautiful girl . . . I checked the local paper and the 'What's on in Willminster' website practically every day to be sure to catch any upcoming gigs. And then bingo! One Saturday I found Jewel was on at this new bistro place in the square. I was beside myself. I roped in Alex, not telling him anything, of course. I'd have been digging my own grave; it'd have been round the school in nanoseconds.

So there we were in Blinkered, this new place, right up front, with Alex moaning about being dragged out to see some pathetic local band and me – well, on the edge, strung out. Wondering what I'd be feeling. Whether it would be the same, or if I'd made some huge mistake. I was feeling like Daniel Prat, even though I was wearing my new, cool Ikos bought especially for the occasion. I felt pathetic and exhilarated at the same time. The story of my life.

The band came out first and played a couple of current hits. There was the buzz of chatter, no one was listening. Then, out walked my girl.

Silence.

I am telling you that bar just stopped dead, as if it'd been turned off, like a radio.

I thought my heart would stop. I even felt a bit faint. Alex was staring, his eyes on stalks. Yeah, of course, she was as gorgeous as I remembered: tiny, fragile, an angel, her hair streaming down her back . . . and everyone else could see it too. And when she started singing, Alex's mouth dropped open.

I sat there in a state of high euphoria as she worked her way through the set. Her voice! It was so full and resonant. I could already hear her singing my song, 'A Voice in the Crowd'. And then they finished and the crowd went wild. And they came back almost at once and I was thinking, it's got to be 'The Tracks of My Tears': it's got to be. And I don't know what happened, but I heard this voice shouting, 'Play "Tracks of My Tears"!' And honestly, it was a few seconds before I realised it was me.

'Who's that?' she was looking out into the audience. 'Who said that?'

'Over here! Here he is!' Alex was pointing at me and shouting.

And she looked at me.

And she smiled. 'Ah, you there at the front . . .'

I could have died right there on the spot!

Then she smiled again, looked at her band. 'OK, boys?' Then back at me. '"Tracks of My Tears", babe, just for you.'

They started up the familiar riff. *'People say I'm the life of the party . . .'* I was trying to be cool. But I was actually shaking, like a cocktail of mortification and excitement. I knew I'd been sussed by Alex. He could hardly contain himself. He thought it was *so* funny. His face was dancing with mirth. Even his dreads had come to life, jangling around his head in glee. But, you know, within seconds the music had taken over. Her voice was like angel dust. I got stuck into the song with her. Silently drumming the chords on the table. And then it was over.

Alex started up as soon as we were out of the door. 'Oh, I see it *now*! That's what all this is about. I knew there was something. All this moony song-writing stuff! Danny's got a crush, Danny's got a cru-ush!' He was dancing around me like a demented monkey.

Do you know something? I didn't care! I'd been noticed. She had *smiled at me*. She had acknowledged my existence. 'Babe, just for you!' Babe! OK. I knew it was too soon; I mean, who was I? Fourteen – never even had a proper girlfriend. I was Nobody. But I was also thinking, nothing is impossible. I had the music in me, man. And there was time.

Everything seemed different. Everything seemed intensified – infused with possibilities. Every song on the radio seemed to relate to how I felt; every girl in every song was Cassie. I was *feeling* different. And for the first time I was feeling the power of my own music. I knew I had a gift – not just for playing music, but writing, and that was the edge. I mean, lots of people can play well, even brilliantly. But not many people can *create* music; good music, music that makes a difference. And I knew deep down I could do that, and the more I worked, the more sure I became, that I had this *thing*, it was flooding out. Like someone had opened a magic door and all these riches were just flowing out into my hands. It was her.

That year I grew a foot. Mum was forced to hand over money for new clothes, and Alex and I went out and bought some really cool stuff. And on the way back from the shops I was crossing the road when I saw this guy walking towards me, tall, cool, *adult-looking* – and then I realised it was me! Daniel Prat That Was. Suddenly, my body had caught up with the rest of me. I felt a small thrill of something, something strong and powerful. Deep down I knew it was to do with Cassie.

Jewel now had a website. I printed off a picture of Cassie and put it in my wallet. Naff, pathetic. But it was good just to look at her face now and again, to remind myself. I went to see the band whenever I could, sometimes with Alex, sometimes alone – I never missed a gig.

What happened next? Well, the prophecy in the local website came true. Alex, who seemed to know everything that was going on in Willminster, told me he'd heard Cassie had got a recording contract. His mum knew someone who knew her mum, sort of thing. I wasn't surprised, but it made me uneasy. She wouldn't be around much longer; she'd be whisked off somewhere. No more local gigs. No more seeing her in the flesh. And what would she be recording? Who'd be writing for her? She needed strong material, she needed my songs. Although it might seem stupid, big-headed, I told myself this. And this could be my last chance.

The local paper did a big double-page splash about her: 'LOCAL GIRL HITS NEW HEIGHTS'. She spoke about how it was all the music for her, and had been since she was small. That she had to sing, sing, sing. How it was everything to her. And that was how I felt. And that was why I knew that some day, music would bring us together. My beautiful, talented girl. There was no one like her.

Not Sandy, my first real girlfriend, a distant cousin of Alex's who I'd met at a barbecue at his parents'. She was sweet and funny. Laughed a lot. I'd been attracted to her because she was small, and dainty, and had long hair, although it was red instead of blond. But it didn't work out; she wasn't Cassie. Then there was Gemma, who sang in the choir. She had a sweet, high, pure voice. We sang harmony together sometimes, sitting in my room, but I couldn't seem to let her in, to that place. There was someone already there.

It was weird. I felt stuck. I just couldn't seem to connect. I felt as if there was only one girl who was right for me, who would understand me. And any time soon she'd be gone, whisked off into another world.

And my songs. I kept them to myself, only occasionally trying something out on Alex – and getting the usual infuriating, teasing response, but in his roundabout way he let me know what he felt. I knew, if I was going to do that thing, that I'd have to test them soon. Try them out on real, live people.

So, back to the concert. By that time I had a whole catalogue of songs, and all of them for her. Love songs. Three of them were good. Very good. These were the three I picked to launch on the world. And the response was more than I could have hoped for. It was time.

A small club in London. I was waiting. I got the date on the Internet. Banham's, famous for showcasing up-and-coming bands. Cassie Tyler and support. I had spent hours getting ready. Studying myself in the bathroom mirror. Giving myself the critical eye. One minute I felt like Daniel Prat, the next I felt like cool, singer-songwriter, Daniel Banks. Hey! I tried to gee myself up. Black T-shirt, my scuffed, faded jeans. I gelled my hair back. Flat, dark curls. OK, I wasn't drop-dead – I knew that – but I felt serious and cool. The musician.

I got the six fifty-four to Waterloo. The envelope in my inside jacket pocket. Three songs – lyrics and a CD. I'd recorded them at home, over and over, until they were as perfect as I could get them. Just guitar, voice, and a drum accompaniment. My best work. I could hear her voice singing: '*A voice in the crowd / I knew it was you.*' I knew Cassie didn't write her own stuff, and the few original songs in her set were weak. She needed some strong, original material for her album. I had those songs, right there in my pocket.

The club was already quite full. I hadn't been anywhere like this before. I felt edgy and out of my depth. Of course, I shouldn't even have been allowed in – not yet eighteen – but I was tall and fairly well-built. I bought a ticket – then cruised right in without a second glance from the doorman. A lone guitarist was playing an opening set. I pushed my way to the front and waited. Didn't even bother (or was too nervous) to get a drink. I'd been close to her before, but that night I felt a fusion of fear and elation brewing in my stomach. This was it.

The band came out first and played a few bars of intro. Then she came out wearing a pale-blue dress, cut low in the front and covered with tiny spangles. She looked stunning – but small and vulnerable too. I imagined us together. I imagined her folding against me. As she started to sing, I felt a hollow forming in my chest. It was so huge, what I was doing. Daniel Berk. I wasn't sure I could go through with it. I wasn't sure at all.

It was a stunning set. The audience went mad, whooping

and whistling. They came back for an encore. She did two more songs, but I hardly knew what they were. I couldn't take my eyes off her. She finished with that little movement with her hands – as if she was about to fly, to take off.

I had this fantasy, you see. That she'd take my songs and listen to them right away. She'd telephone me with an invitation to meet. I'd be cool – no betrayal of feelings . . . yet. Girls didn't like that, I knew. Didn't like you to be too keen straight off. Then, gradually, as we worked on the songs, the arrangements, she would fall in love with me. And then the first kiss. And that would be it. Nirvana.

I waited a few minutes. My plan was to go backstage, ask for an autograph, then to mention, casually, our home town – get her into conversation. I was thinking she might even recognise me, from all the gigs I'd been to. But then, just as I was getting up my nerve, I saw her walking out the stage door, by herself, walking up to the bar. Changed now, into a black halter-top that showed off her lovely back, and jeans, her hair streaming down her back. My heart was pounding. Now my chance had come, it felt ridiculous. *I felt ridiculous.* It seemed impossible that she was just *there,* like an ordinary, everyday person, waiting to be served. Everyone was turning to look at her. You know, I actually felt *jealous.*

I went to the bar. The envelope in my pocket seemed to press against my chest, to burn like something alive. I took it out and laid it face down on the counter. My hands were shaking. The rest of the band would be out any minute. Do it! Do it, Daniel, before it's too late!

'Hi.'

She turned, looking startled. Then she smiled. 'Hi.'

'That was a great set!' It came out too loud, too enthusiastic. Prat.

'Why, thanks, babe. Glad you enjoyed it. It's a new set I'm working on, for my album.'

'Yeah, I heard you'd been signed. Fantastic!'

'Thank you again, babe—' she put her head on the side '—do I know you?'

I was practically hyperventilating. I had to give her that envelope. It seemed like the hardest thing I would ever do.

'I'm from Willminster,' I said, trying to keep my cool. 'I've seen the band a few times. Saw you first at the summer fair.'

She laughed. A deep, throaty laugh, which, like her voice, was startling coming from someone so small. 'Oh, yeah, babe. Those were the days.' She was looking around, towards the stage door. I felt I was losing her. Do it, Daniel. Do it.

'I'm a songwriter,' I blurted out. I picked up the envelope. Now or never.

'Oh yeah, babe?' But she was really looking distracted now. I couldn't blame her. Strangers must approach her all the time. Weirdos, creeps. I had to make it clear somehow that I wasn't a nerd. That I knew my stuff. 'I play a bit myself. Local mostly.' A slight exaggeration – Alex's bedroom and the school concert – but still . . .

'Really?' She wasn't even looking at me now but the nearness of her was flooring me.

'Yeah. I've got these songs, actually.' I held the envelope towards her. I had never felt so nervous. Never in my whole life. 'I was wondering if you'd like to listen to them? They're lyrics and a CD. If you were interested . . . I mean, if you think you could use them . . . I mean, I'm not interested in a deal myself. I'm a writer, really. These songs, well, people say they're good – that they ought to be recorded . . .'

She looked at the bartender. Did she roll her eyes?

The stage door opened. The guys from the band tumbled out, with a couple of girls – hangers-on.

She turned. I had to move then, or never.

I tapped her on the shoulder. I knew I was probably going too far. 'Here, have them. You can always chuck them away.'

She turned back. Her smile was colder now. But she took the envelope. She had it in her hands!

I walked away. Exhausted. Drained. I sat down at a table, my heart still pounding. I was suddenly aware of the sweat, sticky under my arms. God! My whole body was rattling with nerves. I was cringing. Half with embarrassment ('I'm a writer, really . . .' did I say that?) half with elation. She had the envelope. My songs.

I suddenly became aware that I was staring at her. That was no good. I didn't want her to think I was some kind of crazy stalker, if she didn't think that already. I glanced around the room, although I wasn't really seeing anything. Then I chanced a trip to the Men's. I hardly dared look in the mirror, just in case I looked pale, weird, like I felt inside. But it was OK. The guy looking back at me was just me, Daniel, in my black T and jeans. Cool. Finally, I felt a sense of elation. I'd done it!

I made my way back to the table. When I looked up at the bar, they were gone.

Still. Mission accomplished. Cassie Tyler had my songs. My mouth felt like sandpaper, it was the nerves. I went back to the bar. It was ten o'clock. I'd have a Coke and get the ten forty-five home.

I leant against the bar, beginning to feel life oozing back into my bones. It was a good feeling, I felt light, weightless. I looked down the length of the counter at the debris of their little party – glasses, an ashtray, an empty cigarette packet–

– and a small, brown envelope.

Told myself she was distracted, all hyped up after the gig. Easy to put something down and then forget. I'd done that myself. But all the elation I'd felt drained away on the way home. Gloom. Doom. What had that cost me, eh, to do that? I'd never been anywhere like that club before in my life. I felt sick. But then again I told myself I'd made contact. Hey! I'd send her the songs. She'd remember me, for sure, what with the Willminster connection. So I got on to Google and found out the name of her record company. I wrote a letter – short, to the point – reminding her of our meeting, saying a bit about the songs. And looking forward to hearing from her.

Funny, ha ha. Six months later I got a package with a photocopied letter. '*Miss Tyler thanks you for your correspondence, but because she receives such a large amount of mail she is unable to answer personally. However, she has signed this photograph for you.*' The songs were returned, the paper pristine, the seal on the CD unbroken.

Was I gutted? Yes, and more. But I told myself she must get a lot of mail, heaps. She probably doesn't even get to look at it herself. I buried it. Deep. I had all this excess energy. So

Mum got her way. I threw myself into work. Working for that scholarship. I played piano until my fingers dropped off. Alex said the other day, 'You are boring the pants off me, man!' I wasn't arguing. I needed to do well at this. Bach, Chopin, Mozart – I worked myself silly by day, and wrote my own stuff at night. One day Mr Devonish called me in and said he thought I had a really good chance of the scholarship. '*Really* good, Daniel.' Mum was over the moon. I was thinking, I could if I wanted to. Do I want to? Dunno. The important thing was that I *could*.

Cassie's album came out. Rave reviews. But they were all about her voice. I bought it on day one and listened to it in the dead of night, lying on my bed, lights out. The voice, thrilling – what else? – but there was something missing. Just two original songs, the rest of it covers, and 'The Tracks of My Tears', of course . . .

Then came the day that everything changed. And it was Alex who started it all. Alex got me a gig at the summer fair – where I'd first seen Cassie. I was nervous. Playing at school was one thing. Playing to hordes of uninterested Saturday-afternoon shoppers could be suicide. But he went on and on about it and finally I caved in. He'd been acting strange about the whole thing. I couldn't figure it. Kept saying how important it was that I perform well, asking what songs I was going to do – even what I was going to wear! In the end I just said, 'Leave off, man! What's all this about?'

'Nothing, mate. Just want you to do well. And remember, *don't sing with your eyes closed!*'

The gig was a blinder (no pun intended) although, yeah, I couldn't help it, I didn't look at the audience. I played the whole set – five songs – with my own stuff. A gamble, because people usually like stuff they know, that they can sing along to. But I got them, I felt it, the ripple of energy coming back at me. And after every song, the little gaggle of girls at the front grew bigger. I was thinking, if only *she* were here to see this!

Afterwards, Alex came loping over grinning from ear to ear. He had this man with him. I knew at once he was someone important: flash clothes, brown leather shoes, lace-ups that looked like they cost a fortune, an air of confidence.

Joseph Frayn. A music publisher, quite well-known. I was stunned. Alex had sent him a CD of my stuff. He was interested in me, he said. Interested in my writing. I was nervous as hell, but elated. This guy, this important guy, had come all the way from London – to see me!

That was the beginning of it all. Mum went ballistic. 'Who is this man? What about your studies? The scholarship!' I was throwing away a brilliant future for some dodgy deal; I was wasting my 'God-given gift'. But I persuaded her I could do *both*. 'No reason why I can't write alongside my studying,' I smooth-talked. I knew this was a once-in-a-lifetime chance. I was going with it.

I signed a contract with Joseph's company. He was free to offer the songs, all except *those three*. 'Why?' he asked, 'they're very strong.' I told him it was personal.

Of course, I didn't expect it to come to anything – not so soon, anyway. I was just ordinary Daniel Banks. Living in a suburban town with his mum; studying for his exams. Messing around with Alex. But then I got this phone call, out of the blue. An ex-member of a famous boy band –

going solo – liked a couple of my songs. A double-sided single was on the cards.

I took a deep breath and fell back against the wall. My very first thought wasn't to ring Alex, or even to tell Mum. It was that this would bring me one step closer to Cassie. This was the beginning, surely.

Things moved quickly. The single came out to good reviews. Then all of a sudden I heard it had shot up to number seven in the charts, practically overnight, and it was to be on *Top of the Pops*. Me and Alex, Mum, and a couple of friends watched it on our TV. To see my music sung by someone else, my words, in this big arrangement, it was amazing, unreal. And more unreal, Cassie Tyler was on the same show. It made me weak. She would be listening, hearing *my* words, not knowing they were about *her,* like every song I ever wrote.

Joe rang. This was amazing, he said. The beginning. I'd have to start thinking about my future.

When I walked into assembly the next morning everyone turned to look at me. I don't think anyone had actually believed it before last night. I had wanted to keep it quiet, but of course Alex had managed to put it around. There was a buzz; people I didn't even know talked to me. Little gaggles of girls seemed to be everywhere, whispering and giggling. I even got a couple of love notes. The following week, set up by Alex, the *Willminster Gazette* came to interview me. When the piece came out, 'LOCAL BOY HAS TOP TEN HIT', it seemed like an echo; an echo of Cassie's journey. I was catching up. Even Mum was a bit impressed, although she went on about it not going to my head. About how my *real* future was with the piano. But already I was changing. Already I knew I would take a different path.

And Cassie? I don't know why I hung onto her. But I did. It's like your first love lodges itself in your gut and won't budge. The image of her, that first time at the summer fair, was like a blueprint of some fantastic design that could never be copied. I still thought about her every day. Her voice, the way she looked. The way we would be together, sharing our music. The way she would fit so perfectly in my arms. But even with this first success, I was feeling that maybe whatever I did would never be enough. Her album was doing well; she was appearing on television now and again. Saturday-morning kid shows. This young singing sensation. I still logged on to the website every day; followed her every move.

And another girlfriend, Claire. She was really sweet, and I almost fell in love with her, but it was like I had a lock on my heart and the only person in the world who had a key was Cassie – the exact combination – voice, hair, eyes, height, hands, feet.

It was the run-up to Christmas. The fuss about my single had died down a bit and I was still working hard on my piano but something had changed. I knew I had a future as a songwriter. The desire to please Mum and Mr Devonish was fighting with my true passion. My real purpose for being on earth.

Cassie's second album, *Princess*, came out the week before Christmas. It wasn't so great. There were more original songs, but they were weak, insipid, contrived. It came in way down in the charts and then sank. She was slipping out of public consciousness. She needed stronger material.

And me? I had a gift for the 'middle eight', Joe said – that chorus that hooked you and embedded itself in your mind. Very soon, Joe had got another deal. A big name this time. Real big. Mum's face was a picture when I told her. Anxiety, disappointment, excitement – worry – pride. I could read her like a book. She didn't want to be too enthusiastic, she wanted to keep my feet on the ground; she wanted me to go on with the scholarship. Did she? In the end she started crying. I think it was beginning to hit home.

Alex just said, 'Well, that's more like it, Danny Boy. Bit more like the real thing.'

Fast forward. Two years later. London. I'm living with Joe and his wife, Marcie. I've had two number ones. And my latest, with a new girl band, climbing the charts in America. This morning there was a piece about me in *NME*: 'Young Daniel Banks seems to have some kind of magic, alchemy, the way he keeps coming up with hit after hit. He even seems to know what is coming next!' Joe laughed. 'You're a prophet, baby Daniel!' It was unreal. Made my head spin.

Then it happened. A phone call. A deep confident voice, authoritative. Cassie Tyler's agent. Did I know her work? I wanted to laugh. 'Yeah,' I said, shaking inside. 'Great voice.'

The agent went on. Cassie wanted to make a new album, but she needed a big song, a few big songs actually, to secure the deal. 'I'd like to come by,' she said, 'hear what you've got, maybe see if you could write something for her? She's a big admirer of yours, huge. I mean she loves what you've done for The Angels. We were really impressed, both of us. Can we fix a time – maybe next week?'

'She's got to come herself.'

'Well . . .'

'I only see artists in person – that's the way I know whether the song will fit.'

'Oh, but I don't know, she's very busy.'

'So am I.'

There was a long silence. Princesses don't talk to frogs; they send their handmaidens to do it.

'Well, I don't know . . . perhaps, I mean, I could come by any time – to suit you – go through your stuff – and then if there was something – maybe then—'

'I'm sorry, that's not the way I work. If you change your mind . . .' I made as if to finish the conversation, the phone was going down . . .

'Well, OK. I'll see what I can do.'

I was at the studio, standing in the window, watching the car. Three people emerged, a woman – the agent, I guessed, and two guys, one reaching inside to help someone out. Cassie's entourage. No celebrity travelled without an entourage, a team – it was a status thing. It made them feel they were up there, like royalty with their courtiers. Cassie appeared from the back seat, like some exotic bird from a gilded cage. I buzzed them in.

I'd dressed carefully that morning. Nothing flash. Black T-shirt, with my logo RSONGS, jeans, and understated pair of Nikes. Pretty much what I'd been wearing at our last meeting. I saw my reflection in the window. Was I still

Daniel Prat? I didn't know. I was somewhere in between.

The agent came in first, smiling, hand outstretched. Then the two guys, introduced as her new backing musicians. And then Cassie Tyler. A proper entrance for a princess. Long coat, like a cloak, a little wispy top made of some gauzy material that clung to her. High, high heels, her lovely hair pinned up. I half expected a page to follow, carrying a bejewelled crown on a velvet cushion. I stood up – my heart was thumping like a drum. Bang, bang, bang. She was here, in my studio, right in front of me, smiling. How different this was, this second time. She looked at me quizzically as she shook my hand. 'Hey babe, do I know you? You look familiar.'

I had expected this.

'Oh, you've probably seen me around, at some press thing – some party.'

Her hand in mine, tiny, delicate, but surprisingly strong.

They sat back on the couch. I reached for the demo – the very same CD that had been left on the counter, among the debris, like rubbish.

The little entourage were chatting among themselves. I went to slot in the CD but changed my mind. I'd play live. I picked up my Gibson and began to tune . . .

When I came to the end of the first song, 'A Voice in the Crowd', she began to join in. Her sweet, earthy voice pitched perfectly in harmony. It was hardly believable; after all these years, my fantasy was coming true. It was thrilling.

I reached the end. They all applauded.

Cassie was out of her seat. 'Wow, babe! Where did *that* come from? I've *got* to have it! It's *fantastic*! Has anyone else heard it, babe? No one else is considering it, are they?'

She was looking at her agent, as if to say, '*Do something.*' The agent was pale. I knew what she was thinking. A killer song. A number one for Cassie.

It was all in my power.

It was thrilling.

Thrilling that the subject of the songs was sitting in front of me, and she didn't even know it.

I said nothing. I played the other two songs. They clapped and wowed and whooped.

'Well?'

Cassie started to speak. All hyped up. The agent motioned her to be quiet. She would handle this.

Cassie rang me four times. The agent – I lost count. I didn't know what was wrong with me. I couldn't seem to respond, one way or the other. Didn't even tell Joe what was going on. Kept putting them off. Someone else had come on the scene, I said. It was a difficult decision. Of course, I'd always loved Cassie's voice, but now there was another offer. The agent was demented, said they would match any offer, Cassie was wild about the songs. But I was frozen.

One day I came home to find my answerphone buzzing with messages. Cassie. Her voice still did something to me, reached somewhere inside. She was inviting me to a dinner, at her house. So-and-so would be there, and him and her. Big names. '*Hope you can make it, babe.*' She wanted to see me, not just for business, but for fun – she was saying, too lightly, a little laughing note in her voice. Nerves. I knew that feeling.

Time passed. I stopped returning the calls. I sold the songs, my best and truest work, to a big new American artist. A young singer, a sensation, only sixteen. All three were included on her second album. 'A Voice in the Crowd' shot straight to number one, in the UK too.

Why? I knew Cassie would be thinking the same thing.

Maybe I just didn't like the way she kept saying 'babe'.

Two more years passed. I was sitting in the kitchen, drinking coffee and reading the *Mirror*, entertainment pages. There was a tiny piece at the foot of the page. Cassie Tyler – once pop's princess, fallen from grace – now playing small out-of-town clubs. There was a smudgy photograph.

I felt nothing but a sort of distant coldness. Almost cruel. Not like me at all. But what *am* I like? I'm like everyone else, with a dark place somewhere that never forgives. And that's so deep down, *you don't even know it's there.*

I rang Alex, now at uni in London. Then put on my jacket and walked out into the Soho night to meet him, feeling as if something I had been carrying around all my life – a heavy, draining weight – had been lifted.

This story was inspired by 'The Swineherd'. CC

The Shattered Mirror

Aurora was wounded: Kieron had shot her a glance full of scorn. Kieron, her childhood friend, the boy who'd been her reflection, her shadow, her alter ego all these years. Tears that were nothing to do with the frosty air sprung to her eyes, forcing her to turn her face so he couldn't see them. She walked away through the snow. Kieron didn't call her back.

She'd done nothing different, said nothing unusual; simply smiled the warm, bright-eyed smile that lit up her pretty, freckled face when she'd chanced upon him standing at the top of the slope with his sledge. But Kieron was taller these days, cleverer, and Aurora's lifelong loyalty was no longer enough.

Kieron watched her go. He wasn't sorry. There was something about Aurora that irritated him even now as she trudged away through the snow, her stripy scarf fluttering forlornly, her long brown curls trailing down her back. He leapt onto his sledge and sped down the hill, slicing through the whiteness to the gully below.

Aurora lay curled up on the sofa, sadly remembering the good times. As babies she and Kieron had shared baths and beds; as children, stories and parties. They'd ridden their bikes and swum in the lake in summer and sledged on the hill in winter. They'd walked to school together, taken the bus together when they got older. They'd understood one another utterly, playing wordless games or dressing up and putting on plays. Once they'd tried to run away together, packing a suitcase that contained nothing more than their pyjamas and a complete set of the Narnia Chronicles.

Narnia had been their joint obsession, equalled only by Lyra's adventures a year or so later. The good and evil of those snowy scenes were lodged for ever in their souls. Aurora sighed. One year they'd played White Witch with their friends in the playground to the exclusion of all other games. Catch and touch and freeze. Catch and touch and freeze. Only Aslan could set you free. Only the warm breath of the lion Aslan could bring you back to life. Kieron always wanted to be Aslan. Then.

It wasn't that Aurora was in love with Kieron. It wasn't like that at all, which was why she was so hurt by his rejection. It was as if he'd suddenly seen her differently; failed to recognise his oldest friend somehow. It was as if ice had taken hold of his heart, he'd been so cold.

Aurora went over to the mirror above the fireplace and peered at her face. It hadn't changed overnight. The same brown curls with glints of spun gold. Same deep-set, bright, brown eyes with white whites and dark lashes that brushed the dusting of freckles on her cheekbones. Same sweetly curved lips. And she imagined Kieron in the mirror behind her, her mirror image, her opposite with his fairish hair, straight as straw, and the grey-blue eyes now turned to steel. But he wasn't there.

When Kieron regarded himself in the mirror these days it was with a critical eye. His face had grown longer, his eyebrows heavier, his hair more inclined to greasiness. Spots appeared overnight. He didn't like what he saw there. He was taller, paler, sweatier. He knew his hormones were running riot. Thoughts of Aurora unsettled him: she had been his friend all this time, but she was a *girl*, and that no longer made sense. Friends and girls affected him differently. Right now there was a girl called Kristel who fascinated him – him and all the boys in his class. She'd landed a snowball on his cheek back when he was sledging. He could feel it still, ice and fire at the same time.

Kieron took off his wet clothes. His skin had broken out particularly badly this winter and he saw in the shower that his shoulders and back were covered in unpleasant lumps and bumps. There was even a lump in his armpit. Kieron felt it when he rolled on his deodorant. He dressed and went down to sit at the kitchen table with the crossword. Kieron could always lose himself in word puzzles. They took his mind off more troublesome things.

A week later the acne on Kieron's back had subsided as

acne does, but the lump in his armpit was still there. He told his mother and she made him an appointment with the doctor who immediately sent him to the consultant at the hospital. So there sat Kieron, with his mother in the white waiting room, wondering quite calmly what was to become of him. He gazed into the whiteness of the walls and lost himself in the calm image that comforted him above all others – a lamppost in the snow, standing in the dark Narnian forest beyond the wardrobe, with a halo around the light and the white flakes drifting gently down and down for ever.

Kieron had cancer. Hodgkin's. His chances were quite good. *Snowflakes drifting in the lamplight.* Chemotherapy was unpleasant but effective. *The trees glistened in the forest.* And there were other treatments too, nowadays. If all else failed they could try one of these. You do understand, don't you, Kieron? *Somewhere deep in the forest lurked the White Witch. Catch, touch, freeze.* Kieron shivered. 'I understand,' he said, and briskly rubbed at the goose bumps that had risen on his arms.

In the days that followed, Kieron came to dread the look reflected in other people's eyes. So many times his mother had to turn her face away to hide her tears. His father too. It made Kieron angry. He was coping, why weren't they?

When Aurora was told, a whiteness filled her head. She lay on her bed and punched the pillow again and again, but it didn't help. She wanted to rush round and hug her friend, but she knew she was no longer welcome.

*

Kieron had chemotherapy. His father sat with him and clenched his fists as the poison filled his son's veins and turned him white like stone. Kieron tried to conjure up images of polar bears by the frozen lake, upright and proud, ready to fight. But he felt weak as a flapping fish impaled on a polar bear's claw.

When Kieron wasn't too tired he went into school. He wore a baseball cap to cover his downy head. His face looked like marble, and gleamed with a strange glamour. Kristel, one-time object of Kieron's fantasies, now found herself weirdly drawn to him, as if by a powerful magnet. She started to hang around him. Aurora watched from a distance.

Kieron had no resistance to infections any more. When he was ill he was rushed to hospital and he wanted to cry out in frustration and fear. He gritted his teeth and smashed his fist against the wall to create a pain he knew would go away. His father hugged him fiercely. 'My darling boy. It can't go on like this. It won't.' Kieron avoided his eyes because of the abyss that lay behind them.

For a while Kieron disappeared into the dazzle of pain and terror. Aurora decided to visit him regardless, but when she arrived she found Kristel there at his bedside, queen of the white sheets and mountainous pillows. Kieron barely acknowledged Aurora. She left him puzzle books and CDs and melted back, half grateful, into the vibrantly-coloured land of the living.

Kieron's life in hospital became one huge, pain-filled Christmas. The boxes emptied, the gifts piled up. E-book, iPod, PlayStation 2. No expense was spared. What price a few moments of happiness for a dying boy? Visitors would discover Kieron plugged into an endless computer game of other worlds, oblivious to the hospital around him. He barely spoke, not even to Kristel. No one knew what went on in his head.

Except Aurora. She knew because Kieron was part of her. She knew the battle he was fighting and that he feared the touch of the White Witch above all else. *Catch, touch, freeze.* Anything to keep her at bay – games, puzzles, even the vacuous Kristel, it seemed. Aurora prayed for Kieron to win the battle, to embrace a future that wasn't death. A future awash with colour and light, great curtains of gorgeous-coloured light that billowed over the landscape, green and blue and purple and rose. Somewhere in Kieron's head the Northern Lights must be encouraged to swirl and promise life.

Though she knew she wasn't wanted, Aurora persuaded herself to keep on visiting Kieron with yet more books and music. Kieron was bald and his skin was waxy yellow. His eyes were dark slits. The White Witch couldn't be far away. He turned his back on Aurora and carried on with his computer game.

The images weren't working for Kieron any more. What was snow falling round a lamppost? What was a polar bear by a frozen lake? What use was such constancy? Though Kieron knew they were part of him, his psyche, such symbols couldn't help him now. They belonged to a time with Aurora – in the past. The present was Kristel. To her credit, she was nearly always at Kieron's bedside. She'd become part of his white hospital world. She seemed to revel in her association with him, the boy at death's door.

Kristel didn't really have other friends, or even much personality. She was all radiance and no core.

It was winter again. Kieron sat at home glued to his computer screen. His latest scan at the hospital had not been good. The chemotherapy wasn't working and the doctors were resorting to a different treatment. Sometimes Kieron wished he was dead, wished he'd got the dying over with. Kristel hovered, beautiful but hollow. Was Kieron beginning to tire of her?

One freezing evening Aurora saw Kristel leaving Kieron's house and made up her mind to pay him a visit, make him take notice of her. She gathered up some magazines and DVDs and knocked on his door. Kieron's father let her in and she could see Kieron round the corner in his baseball cap clicking away furiously at his PlayStation control.

'Hi,' she said. Kieron grunted and carried on playing. At least he hadn't completely ignored her. Aurora looked around at the heaped-up boxes of computer games threatening to overwhelm the room. Her gaze came back to rest on her old friend's tense and skinny back. She watched his gaunt and bony frame jerk beneath his T-shirt as his thumbs wiggled and clicked away, and her heart nearly broke.

Without thinking, she stumbled over to where he sat and threw her arms around him. 'Oh, Kieron!' she sobbed, and hot tears ran down her face. Caught by surprise Kieron looked into her brimming eyes, and there was no abyss there. No fear or pity – just love. And tears started to glisten on his cheeks too, as the pair of them clung together.

'Are you all right to come outside for a bit?' asked Aurora, blowing her nose. 'If you wrap up warm? Have you got the energy?'

'Suppose so,' he replied. 'I'll never crack that game anyway.'

So they went out into the cold, cold evening. As they spoke, the words on their warm breath turned into ice, mingled, and hung in the air. Kieron looked at Aurora in her rainbow-coloured scarf with her glinting curls and her bright eyes. 'You're so warm,' he said.

Aurora smiled her sweet smile. 'The new treatment is going to work, Kieron. You're going to get better,' she said fiercely, stopping beneath the streetlamp to hug him tightly, and wrapping him right round with all the glorious bright colours of her scarf. So when they looked up into the halo around the light and saw the first snowflakes falling, it was impossible for Kieron not to kiss her.

This story was inspired by 'The Snow Queen'. KP

A Little Flame

Maddy was in Paris! Paris! One minute she'd been slumping around their tiny London flat with nothing to look forward to except four days (a prison sentence, Maddy thought) at Gran and Gramps's overheated little house in Stevenage, eating too much and watching endless game shows. Then, on the day before they were due to pack up and head off on the journey of doom, as Maddy called it, Mum's best friend Lucy had rung up from France to say her husband had left her, just like that. Up and gone. Run off with a woman he'd met at the gym, and she hadn't even had a clue! They were in the same boat, she said, her and Mum. And she wanted Mum to come out for the holidays. Even though Maddy's mum insisted they couldn't possibly afford it, Lucy went on and on about how it wouldn't cost them anything but the fare and she had a *whole feast* of food she'd got in for *his* family and that there was no way she was going to sit staring at it, crying into it, all by herself. It would only be thrown away.

So now Maddy was in Paris. At Christmas. And it was, she thought, the most magical time of her life.

Maddy stood at the corner of the street with an armful of French bread. Baguettes, as you called them here. You bought them fresh every morning and ate them with big cups of strong, milky coffee which made Maddy's heart race, but she didn't care. She wanted to do everything the French way – even dipping her bread in her coffee, like Lucy did, though Mum said it was disgusting.

Every morning she went to fetch the bread and she loved it. She was hardly allowed past the front door on her own at home, even though she was thirteen going on fourteen. But here they were happy for her to walk all the way to the baker's – and it was *brilliant*. Maddy felt entirely herself in the early-morning street, with the shops opening and people saying *Bonjour* to her – complete strangers, smiling at her, and the *smell*: coffee and bread and something heady and sweet that she couldn't name. Maybe excitement.

On the third morning, the baker said, '*Ah, la petite Anglaise!*' when she arrived, which made her blush, but also feel proud, like she belonged, and she said, '*Trois baguettes, s'il vous plaît,*' and then, feeling encouraged, added, '*Monsieur,*' and was rewarded with a huge grin and a little sticky pastry thrown in free, so by the time Maddy left she was feeling an unfamiliar little bubble of joy in her chest. No one back home was nice to her like that. In fact, no one seemed to notice her at all.

And that was another thing. The boys! French boys seemed to look at you. Not in a leery, mocking way, but properly. Straight into your eyes. Yesterday, a boy had smiled at her. Actually smiled straight at her!

All this was going through her head as she gulped down the sweet pastry, making her way past the chocolate shop, the newsagent and the florist, where an ancient lady in black with her hair pulled back in a tight bun was filling pails with holly and mistletoe. She smiled at Maddy and said, '*Bonjour, Mademoiselle*,' making her feel, again, like she was someone special. A special little English girl walking down the boulevard on this cold, sharp but brilliantly sunny, French morning.

Then, as she was passing an old, derelict building on the corner of an alley, Maddy heard a noise. It was a high-pitched little whine and at first she thought she had imagined it. She stopped for a second. There it was again! A sad, scared noise, coming from somewhere in the alley. Maddy's first thought was: an animal. A small animal, maybe a puppy, a cat, or even a kitten, trapped somewhere. She stood, almost frozen, not knowing what to do. Both Lucy and Mum had made her swear to come straight back – no wandering off – and something told her that walking down a deserted alley all by herself was stupid, even in broad daylight. So she walked on, but then she stopped again. What if a kitten was trapped somewhere, cold and hungry? She could give it some bread, and there couldn't be any real danger, could there? She retraced her steps. If I hear it again, she told herself, I'll go and look. If I don't, I'll just go home and forget it.

Then she heard a sort of scrambling and scratching that definitely sounded like a little animal. It *is*! she thought. It's a kitten!

As soon as she entered the alley she knew she'd made a terrible mistake. It was narrow and very dark, hardly enough room to turn around. Then a terrible stench hit her, like urine and dampness mixed up with something harsh and bitter. It stung her nostrils and made her eyes smart and she felt a sudden wave of fear. What if someone came in behind her? She wouldn't be able to escape. Further down, in the murky light, she saw a gap to the right, like a little side turning. The back of the old building. It's there, she thought. Whatever it is, is *there*.

A row of garages were set into a wall, with what looked like some deserted flats above them – dark windows, some draped with bits of dirty cloth. She stepped forward, and then stopped, paralysed with shock and fear. She was looking straight into the face of a girl.

A scrawny girl with matted hair and a filthy shawl around her shoulders; hands encased in those funny gloves with the fingertips cut off. As soon as Maddy appeared, she shot backwards like a terrified animal.

'It's OK,' said Maddy. 'It's only me,' she added, feeling stupid.

Beside the girl was an old, rusty tin drum with holes punched out of the sides – the remains of a fire smouldering, and behind her, a big heap of filthy rags. Maddy was frozen. She had never seen anything like this before. She felt pinpricks of fear in the tips of her fingers.

The girl stretched out her hand. '*Pain! Pain!*' she hissed urgently. Maddy understood from her schoolgirl French, but she had guessed anyway what the girl wanted. She broke off half a baguette and handed it to her. The girl immediately began to eat, tearing at the bread with her teeth and gulping it down in huge bites. In a second it was gone.

Maddy gave her the second half. The girl turned and shook the bundle of rags behind her. Amazingly, the pile grunted and then began to move. A hand appeared first, the cracked skin ingrained with dirt. And then a head of thick, wild, grey hair, and then a face, unlike any Maddy had seen before, poked out and stared straight at her. Dark eyes, sallow skin, broad, long nose, a wide mouth which seemed to stretch from ear to ear and a look of such utter sadness and despair that Maddy felt something turn over in her chest, just as it did when she was watching something really sad on television. The girl spoke to the man in a strange language. Unlike the girl, he took the bread slowly, and began breaking it in little pieces.

'*Mon père*,' said the girl. Then she smiled.

It was as if the sun had come out. Her teeth were small, perfect and white and for a split second her green eyes, the colour of glass, sparked with light and humour. And in that second Maddy saw herself in this strange girl, herself and all of her friends, thirteen going on fourteen. And she saw they were the same.

'*Vôtre nom?*' said Maddy, dredging up the words from the depths of Miss Carter's French class. If only she'd paid more attention!

'Ava,' said the girl, '*et toi?*'

'Maddy, Madeleine,' said Maddy.

'Mad-lane,' repeated Ava.

Then the man moved as if to get up, and Maddy felt that fear again. And the stench, which in those few eerie moments had disappeared, drifted around her again like a poisonous mist. A figure appeared from the adjoining garage – a boy, she thought – and behind him a woman. Maddy turned and ran.

And then she was back in the street, where the cold, clear air struck her sharp in the face. Thank God! Safe. Safe. She gulped at the air, but the smell from the alley seemed to follow her, to cling to her clothes. Would they notice, Mum and Lucy? She felt suddenly very guilty; as if she had done something terrible, something very stupid. They would be furious if they knew. She'd have to come up with a believable story. Think. Think.

The whole episode hadn't taken more than a few minutes, so at first no one commented that Maddy had been longer than usual; but Mum, who noticed everything, sniffed as she took the baguettes from her.

'Maddy! What is that smell? Where have you been? You look pale – and only two baguettes! What's been going on?'

Madeleine blushed, but she had her story ready. 'I wasn't looking where I was going and I tripped. Silly, really, on the pavement and I dropped a baguette into one of those drain things. It stank, Mum. It really stank. Horrible . . .' She looked suitably guilty. 'I'm sorry.'

It worked. Mum went on for a bit about how this was a

strange city and she must watch what she was doing. And Maddy thought, *You* don't know; you don't know *anything*. Stupid. Stupid. But she sat down with them to breakfast. The crusty bread, the jam, the big cups of strong, milky coffee. The sun was bright outside the window. The clock in the hall tick-tocked. Everything was the same as yesterday and the day before. Except it wasn't.

Ava watched her father slowly eat his way through the bread. What a weird thing! That girl – English, she thought, or maybe German – with her shiny blond hair and brand-new trainers appearing suddenly out of the gloom like a vision – and with the bread, as if she knew they were hungry. Would she tell? Somehow, Ava knew she would not, for she too had felt that closeness – the silent language of girls who know each other.

And long-ago times came into her mind. I used to be like that! she thought. And she remembered her grandmother taking her to school, in just such weather as this – biting cold, but with clear blue skies, and Ava wrapped up in her puffa jacket and Gran's huge woollen shawl bundled around her head and shoulders; and real leather gloves, and thick socks in the little red boots which she loved. But that was before. In another life, before she came here. It all seemed so long ago it could have been a dream.

Ava shivered. The fire was low, nearly out. She began making it up again. She got it going enough to make them both a cup of strong black tea. She'd need to work extra hard today to get money for the man who brought the fuel. She knew what could happen to people like them, in cold like this. There was the low hum of whispering as the others got themselves ready, rubbing their hands over their tin-drum fires.

Ava stood up and looked at her father. He didn't look good. Be well, she thought selfishly – or at least be OK enough to come with me today. She didn't want to go out with Rosa. But when her father tried to stand, he stumbled, and fell back into the pile of rags. She could see he wouldn't make it. Perhaps tomorrow. His legs were weak; it was the fever. 'You go with Rosa, try to get me some aspirin, or something, anything . . .'

Ava wrapped her father back up in his rags, and then added her own filthy blankets. She no longer noticed the stench; it was part of her and her life here, under these smoke-blackened walls, where keeping alive was the only thing that mattered.

Ava could see Rosa looking sideways at her. She didn't trust that woman; didn't trust her at all. She was all nice when Papa was around, but it was a different story when they were on their own. She spoke to Ava sharply, and only if she had to – to tell her to hand over half her money, to carry the baby, or to fetch something for her.

Ava and Rosa with her little boy Alexi, only two, tucked inside her coat, shuffled, one by one so as not to be noticed, down the alley and out into the bright light of the street. High above, on the third floor by a pretty white balcony, Madeleine sat eating bread and jam and thinking that the world would never be the same again.

Maddy, Mum and Lucy were in a café in St-Michel-du-Près. That morning they'd been to look at the Eiffel Tower which Maddy had found strangely disappointing – a giant piece of Meccano. Mum hadn't wanted to go up (which at least would have been something), saying she had vertigo, which was the first Maddy had heard of it; she just couldn't be bothered. Then to the Arc de Triomphe which Maddy thought was amazing, standing at the top of this impossibly wide boulevard called Les Champs-Elysées which was so alive with lights and life and energy that it seemed as if it could take off at any moment, like a giant spaceship.

Maddy was thinking about Ava. That look, when she'd seen behind all the raggedness and dirt to the person underneath; a girl like her. And Ava even seemed to be *with her*. When a group of boys called out to her, laughing and teasing, she imagined Ava holding on to her arm, giggling – her new friend. And now they were in this so-called famous café, Les Deux Magots, sitting outside, even though it was freezing cold, and in her mind's eye she saw Ava sitting with them, her long hair in a thick plait down her back, clean and shining. With that smile. And Mum and Lucy thinking what a nice girl she was, Maddy's new friend from France.

Feeling uncomfortable and guilty, as if Mum might somehow guess the story behind her question, she asked Lucy if there were many street people in Paris and where did they live and why were they there? And Lucy didn't seem to think it was an odd thing to ask – 'Oh, you mean asylum seekers' – and went on about how they were flooding the city and living in filthy conditions and bothering all the tourists. 'God, a woman in our block was attacked the other day – just because she didn't have any change! People were sympathetic at first, but not any more – not now the city is practically overrun!'

And Maddy said, what about the children, and Lucy said

it was disgraceful, how they used children to beg, steal, and worse, and they were all filthy, lice-ridden — and in fact, she'd meant to mention that they should all take care to keep their bags zipped up and their money out of sight because they were sly and quick and would have you in a second. But she wasn't talking to Maddy now, she was talking to Mum, with that know-it-all face.

Maddy felt her breath catch in her throat. 'But they're only children!' she snapped, all heated. 'They can't help it; it's not their fault!'

And Mum, a bit taken aback, said, 'Hey, watch your manners, missy! Lucy's giving you good advice. You'd not be feeling quite so kindly if they'd swiped your Christmas money, would you now?' She looked at Lucy for confirmation. But Lucy, bored with the conversation now, was on to something else, distracted by a woman in an impossibly expensive-looking leather coat with a big fur collar who was sitting down at a table to their left. She whispered to Mum that it was someone or other that Maddy had never heard of and couldn't care less about, anyway.

Suddenly, Maddy's fantasy of getting Ava back to the flat, of letting her have a bath and wash her hair, giving her some clothes, really nice ones and somehow persuading Lucy and Mum that she could stay for Christmas dinner, now seemed impossible. But Maddy's imagination was working overtime, her eyes darting here and there as if she could somehow find a solution hiding in the Christmas crowd milling about St-Michel-du-Près with their bags and bags of stuff. Maybe Mum and Lucy would go out and leave her alone in the flat? Then it could all be done in secret and she could think of some way of introducing Ava – like, like . . .

'You know what?' said Lucy. 'We may as well have lunch here, eh? A bit expensive but, hey, it's Christmas. Let's treat ourselves.'

Ava followed Rosa at a safe distance, until they got to the Métro where they fell in step. She knew that when they got into the city centre, to Concorde, the big bustling station, Rosa would give her the baby to carry, while they went up and down different carriages begging for money. Ava knew Rosa gave her the baby to make them look more pathetic, and she hated it. She hated it, too, when he weed down her – that horrible, wet stickiness on her clothes, and the snot and gunk all over her neck and shoulder.

They had come here with such high hopes. Papa had got a job, illegally of course, but still a job, earning what seemed like a huge sum each week. And he'd got a place to live – someone from home who had residency had rented him three rooms and a little kitchen, and even a bathroom with hot water! It was a bit dark and damp, but clean enough, and then he'd telephoned for Mum and Ava to come – it would all be fine – they needed to be together. Gran hadn't been sure at all. Oh no, she wanted to keep Ava with her – at least until everything was really settled – and Ava hadn't been sure herself that she wanted to go to this unknown place where she didn't even speak the language, leaving all her friends and her gran who loved her so much.

But then the excitement of it all took over and after a lot of tearful goodbyes they were here, in Paris, and for a while, everything was all right. And then came the rows, her mum and dad. And then the police came and Ava and her papa came back to find the place deserted and Mama gone. Arrested, said a neighbour. And then they were on the run, all the while trying to find out what had happened without giving themselves away. For a little while a friend let them camp out in his living room – but then there was a raid where Dad worked and he couldn't go back for fear of being caught and sent back home. That was when things started going really wrong. Bad luck stalked them like a wolf; and they had ended up sleeping rough in the dusty garages behind the old corn exchange.

Ava had wanted to ring her grandmother. How she had wanted to do that – just to hear her voice; she knew she would help, would send money. But Papa said no, it wasn't fair, and that things would come right eventually, when he got another job. Then they'd have enough money for a flat, and some left over to send to Gran. And Ava asked then, for the last time, why couldn't they just go home? *Please.* Anything was better than this. And Papa had been quiet for a moment, then he said, 'We can't go back, Ava, at least not for a long time–' he looked at her very seriously '– because because of things that have happened. Don't ask questions, all right? Everything will be OK, once I get back on my feet. I promise.'

But for the past few days, Papa had been ill, shivering hot and cold, and sick in the chest with an awful hacking cough, and Ava had been forced to go out with Rosa and her little boy, which she hated. Once they had got separated, and Rosa hadn't even come looking for her. It was only by luck that Ava had recognised where she was and sneaked on board a bus, that she managed to get home at all. But it could be worse, she knew. Some kids were sent out to steal, and bad things happened to them. At least Ava didn't have to do that.

And then they were in the centre, riding the commuter trains, Ava lugging little Alexi, sniffing and wriggling in her arms, going up and down, up and down, saying, '*S'il vous plaît. Pour le bébé*,' and she forgot everything except her determination to make enough to get Papa his medicine, and some fuel to keep them from freezing. Tonight, she would go as always up the steep steps to the big, bustling tourist area where people were noisy and often drunk, which made them careless with their money.

The next morning Lucy said she would fetch the bread because she had to drop something off with a neighbour and so she'd kill two birds with one stone. Maddy was wild with frustration and disappointment. She had been hoping to see Ava again, not going into the alley, but maybe calling out to her from the street. She had planned to buy her a baguette out of her own money, and some chocolate too.

And then Lucy and her mum spent the whole day nattering – on and on about how awful men were, especially their own, the ones who had gone off and left them. Moan, moan, moan. Maddy had heard it all before, all about her terrible dad, who wasn't really so terrible – just stupid sometimes. And his new wife Michelle, who Maddy thought was false and silly, with her twittering little voice, but not quite the 'devil incarnate' as her mum made out. And then the day was gone and they hadn't even been outside. Maddy read her book and watched some old soaps on cable TV, all the time thinking, I wonder what Ava is doing now? And then it was dinnertime. Mum and Lucy started drinking red wine, getting noisy and silly. She hated her mum like this. She glared at them over dinner, but they kept making jokes, snorting with raucous laughter. They hardly noticed she was there. Still, tomorrow was Christmas Eve.

Christmas Eve, they would go to Montmartre. Lucy told them it was an old, bustling area full of nightlife. It would be magical, she said. They could forget about all their troubles and have some fun. They would eat out in a little restaurant, one of her favourites, and then come back and open the presents, the French way. So cosy!

On Christmas Eve, Maddy was once again on her way to the baker. She shivered in spite of her thick coat.

'God, the weather has really turned!' Lucy had said that morning. 'It's cold enough to freeze your socks off! I've never known it this cold. You wouldn't even suppose the heating was on!'

Maddy had stuffed an extra sweater under her coat, her big warm one with the fringe on the collar. Luckily Mum hadn't noticed.

Maddy passed the old building on the corner of the alley. She didn't like to think of Ava in this cold. Still, the sweater would help, a bit.

Monsieur le Boulanger seemed even more cheerful that morning. '*Ah, ma petite Anglaise!*' he called heartily, and then added, in English, 'What would you like, Meess?'

'*Quatre baguettes, s'il vous plaît,*' said Maddy.

'*Four!* OK, OK! *Joyeux Noël!*' he added, handing them to her.

'*Joyeux Noël,*' said Maddy.

Maddy stood by the alley; it was so still and quiet it seemed impossible that there was anyone back there; let alone a whole band of living, breathing human beings. Perhaps they had gone, moved on somewhere warmer, more sheltered. She was scared to venture down again. It had been her idea to call out, but now it came to it, it seemed ridiculous. And it was so quiet – almost impossible to break the silence to yell out loud enough to be heard back there. She tried yelling in a whisper, 'Ava, Ava!' She waited. Nothing. Not even the little mewing sound she'd heard that first time. She walked a short way down the alley, and called again. It was *so* silent. She walked as far as she dared. It was more scary now she knew what was down there than before, when it had been the unknown. What if they laughed at her? What if Ava wasn't even there? She decided on compromise. She pulled the sweater out from under her coat and put it on the ground with the baguette. With luck, Ava would find it first – after all, she was the only one up last time. She pushed them near the corner, a strange little offering – a red jumper and a French stick. 'Happy Christmas, Ava,' she whispered and hurried away.

A few minutes later, old Jacques Binstoc was passing the alley when something bright caught his eye. He shuffled along the alley and stared down at it. He couldn't believe his luck. Breakfast! And a nice red sweater. That would come in really handy now the weather was turning. His Christmas had come early.

Rosa made her hand over a big share of her money – two of us, one of you, she said – but Ava had enough left over (as well as a secret five-euro note a woman had given her, 'Because it's Christmas,' hidden in her boot) to get some aspirin for Papa, and some lemons to make him a hot drink, like her grandmother used to do when she had a sore throat. And she didn't care that the chemist's assistant flinched as she dropped the change into Ava's outstretched hand, careful not to actually *touch* her, as if she were contaminated. She was just grateful not to be turned away.

Ava was dismayed to find Papa worse. He looked terrible. He was sitting up, but still shivering. His skin was a pale mask, almost blue, and shining with sweat. She quickly put the kettle on the stove, made up his lemon drink and gave him the painkillers. 'Don't come too near, sweetie,' he said. 'We don't want you coming down with this too. Who will look after me?' And he tried to smile.

Ava snuggled up to him. Her feet were agony. She took off her boots and socks. Her toes were swollen and red. She rubbed them vigorously, and wiggled them near the fire and they hurt as if knives were jabbing her. She had never been so cold in her life. But most of all, she worried about Papa. He needed as much warmth as he could get. 'Let's call Gran,' she tried again.

'No! And no, no, no, again! Those pills are doing the trick. I'm beginning to feel better already. One more day and I'll be up and about. I've heard about another job, a factory. As soon as I'm well . . . we'll be back on our feet — we'll get a nice place. *Then* we'll ring Gran . . . promise.'

Ava wanted to believe it. But look at them! How would her papa get a job, looking like a tramp? An old man and she, a filthy urchin. Who would rent a flat to *them*?

Others were bustling about, cooking on the tin-can

stoves. Ava boiled up some noodles, almost all they ate these days; they were cheap and filling. She'd get more money tonight, and keep it all, whatever Rosa said. She'd get something nice for dinner tomorrow. Christmas Day! The thought made her eyes fill. Even though they hadn't been rich back then, they had had warm clothes and a home, and had always spent Christmas Day with Gran, eating a roast dinner and pudding. It seemed like a feast now. A banquet! Those days, which seemed so far away, when her mother had been there and everything had been all right. Where was her mother? No one knew, or no one was saying. This cold and struggle made you forget. Sometimes, she couldn't even remember her mama's face.

Tonight she would go out with the lighters to the tourist place. People would be feeling happy and generous – it was Christmas! She'd make enough to buy some proper food, maybe a pizza, or some fried chicken from the takeaway. And she'd keep all her share. She wouldn't care what Rosa said. She'd look after Papa and herself. That was it. That was all there was.

Night had fallen, although it was always dark where they were, always in shadow. The man, Ivan, would come soon with the lighters. You could buy six for a euro, and sell them for fifty cents each, sometimes a euro – or even two. It was a good profit, if you could shift enough. The tourist areas were the best; there were always people who'd forgotten their lighters, or matches, and were desperate for a cigarette. You kept your eyes sharp and approached them as soon as they pulled a cigarette from the pack. And even if they had a light, they might buy one, a spare, only fifty cents. You could make good money if you were clever, and kept your eyes open.

It was definitely getting colder. Ava told Papa to wrap up, and be sure to keep the fire going, or they'd be in trouble. She would go out with Rosa tonight, but she would lose her. She would work on her own. That way it would be fair if she kept all the money.

She pulled her boots back on. Her feet hurt. But she'd ignore that. What else could she do? From the little crack between the buildings she could see the sky was clear as glass, with tiny stars scattered across, like a magician's cloak.

It was a beautiful tree. Maddy had helped decorate it, and now, with the lights on, and presents heaped underneath, it looked spectacular. They were going out, at last. To this place, Montmartre, that Lucy kept going on about. 'Just wait till you see!'

Maddy wanted to wear her short jacket, with her jeans and ankle boots, but Mum kept going on and on about the weather getting colder, too cold even for snow, and insisted she wore her coat, deep blue with the fur collar, which she always found heavy and cumbersome. And she had to take her woolly hat. A hat, how stupid! When I'm old enough, she thought, she won't be able to tell me what to do. I'll do what I want.

Glancing at herself in the mirror, she pulled on the hat. It looked stupid, as she knew it would. It was babyish. It made her look like a little girl again, not the real Maddy who longed to be out in the world with her friends, meeting boys, being cool. She stared at this younger girl, with her flushed cheeks and bright eyes, who was struggling with the battle of making her feelings known, and true, real excitement – that it was Christmas Eve, and that they were going out at night, and afterwards, the presents. She shrugged and stuffed the hat in her pocket.

When Maddy stepped into the square at Montmartre, she felt as if she was walking onto a film set. The Christmas lights were beautiful, the most beautiful Maddy had ever seen. Not grand, and far away, like on Les Champs-Elysées, just pretty and almost near enough to touch. There were entertainers out on the street, singers dressed up in Christmas costumes, and jugglers and mime artists, and street vendors selling everything from little puppets to roasted nuts. Mum gave her two euros and she bought some cashews. Maddy said, '*Merci*,' as the lady smiled at her, really friendly, and Maddy had never felt more special, that special English girl who existed only in Paris.

They ate as promised at Lucy's favourite restaurant. They had a table right by the window so they could watch the world go by. Maddy found she wasn't hungry – she felt full up already, of sights and sounds and excitement that sat like a bubble on her chest. But she ate an omelette, just to keep Mum happy, and was allowed to have half a glass of red wine, which you could in France. Even children could drink wine.

And then, after what seemed like hours of Lucy going on and on about her terrible husband – Maddy thought she'd go mad with boredom – she was at last outside, back in the square waiting with Mum while Lucy paid the bill. 'My treat,' she had said, 'for Christmas.'

A band of people dressed up as jesters were singing

carols and she wandered off to listen, standing for warmth near the brazier where the woman was roasting the nuts. She began to cheer up. It was lovely, with all the people milling about; smiling, happy people – some a bit drunk, joining in with the singing.

It was then Maddy felt something. Something she couldn't name. She turned: some way off a girl was weaving around the square, holding something up to people in the crowd.

Maddy stared. It couldn't be, could it? Surely not. She hurried over, drawn like something on a string. She circled round, trying to peep without being noticed. She didn't want to make a fool of herself. Then the girl was right in front of her.

The two girls looked at each other. For a moment, Maddy still wasn't sure. Then the girl smiled. So sweet. Of course – it was Ava.

'Mad-lane.'

She just couldn't believe it. She had been thinking about Ava almost all the time, and then, when she had forgotten about her – just for a while – in the magic of the square and Christmas Eve – here she was!

Maddy felt exactly as she had when she saw Kirsten in the playground on the first day of secondary school. A sort of recognition. She had known immediately that she and Kirsten would be friends, best friends – and that was how it had turned out. And now it was the same feeling, with this foreign girl with the green eyes and lovely face. I know you, Maddy thought. *I know you*.

'Mad-lane!' said Ava, pulling something out of her pocket. She held up a cigarette lighter. *'Un euro.* You want!'

Maddy didn't know what to do. Was it a joke?

'But I don't smoke!' she said, but with such a funny look on her face that Ava burst out laughing, and then so did Maddy because the idea seemed so ridiculous. 'But have a euro anyway,' she said, digging into her pocket. 'Have three!'

Ava was swamped in a big, man's working jacket. Maddy tried to see if she was wearing the red sweater. '*Jupe?*' she said, knowing at once that it wasn't the right word. Ava must think she was an idiot. 'Red jumper?' she tried again. Pointing to her chest. 'I –left – it – for – you, *pour toi.*' She pulled open her coat and pointed to her own sweater, then pointed to Ava, as if to say, 'You too.'

Ava was looking more and more puzzled. This girl was trying to tell her something about her jacket?

'*Pour toi,*' Maddy tried again. 'With the bread – *le pain?*'

'*Oui, le pain!*' Ava smiled, uncertainly.

'*Madeleine!!*' Her mother's voice came shrieking across the square.

Maddy kept her back turned and pretended not to hear. She felt mortified; ashamed of Mum and Lucy, in their rich-looking clothes, even though she knew she probably looked the same herself. But somehow it was different, her and Ava.

'Come away from there, right now!' shouted her mother.

Although Maddy couldn't see, she knew her mum was striding in that cross way, her arms swinging, like at the park when Maddy was small and wouldn't get off the slide or the swings or come away from whatever good thing she was doing.

'What *are* you doing!' said Mum, glaring at her, fiercely.

'Just a minute,' said Maddy, raising her eyebrows to Ava, as if to say, 'God, what a pain!'

'Just a minute nothing. Come away, right now!' She grabbed Maddy's wrist roughly and pulled. 'For goodness' sake, you have no idea!'

Pulled away like a child! A baby! Maddy was burning with anger and shame. She had been fooling herself she had done something to help. Ava hadn't got the jumper, that was clear. That was awful, awful! She had found Ava again, and now her stupid, stupid mum . . . She tried to pull back, but her mum was too strong.

Ava was smiling still, her hands in their cut-off gloves grasping a bundle of brightly-coloured lighters. 'Mad-lane!' she said. '*Joyeux Noël!*'

'Happy Christmas!' called Maddy. The whole square with its gorgeous lights and magic seemed to disappear. She felt helpless, furious.

They walked for a little while in silence; Mum, Lucy, Maddy.

'Well, I don't know,' said Mum at last, 'what *on earth* you were doing, talking to that . . . that . . . filthy girl. Didn't Lucy warn us? They're gypsies – brats – they'll steal the coat off your back if you're not careful. Did she touch you, Madeleine? You might have picked something up. She's probably crawling with lice.'

'And God knows what else,' added Lucy in her know-it-all voice.

She's just a girl like me, what's the difference? They should worry about her. Why is everyone worried about me, wanting to look after me, to keep me safe, to smile at me and give me chocolate cakes? I've been thinking that it's because I'm young, and everybody cares about you if you are young. But they don't, they don't. Because why don't they care about Ava? She's only the same as me. If I were poor, they'd hate me too.

All this was swimming round and round in Maddy's head. Nothing really made much sense. And she could hear Mum and Lucy going on and on, as if she'd had an encounter with an axe murderer instead of a skinny thirteen-year-old girl.

'And another thing,' Lucy was saying. 'They're so crafty. Work in gangs mostly, but it's the ones who seem on their own you need to watch, because you can bet there'll be another one behind with his hand in your pocket. One to distract, one to steal . . . I tell you, Maddy, you've had a close—'

Mum cut in, 'Yes, my girl – you better learn from . . .'

It was unbearable.

'SHUT UP! SHUT *UP!*'

Mum reared back in shock. Maddy had never spoken to her mother like that, ever.

'You don't know! You don't know *anything*! Just *shut up*! OK?'

'*Well!*' said Lucy, indignantly.

Mum stared at Maddy in disbelief. 'What on earth has got into you . . .'

Ava stood in the middle of the square transfixed. How *weird*. That girl Mad-lane appearing again, out of the thousands and thousands of people in Paris, and then the little scene with that woman. But that didn't upset her, really, because that's how it was. Ava was used to people thinking badly of her. And it didn't matter because she knew they had something between them, her and Mad-lane. And she dared to think: she *likes* me. She really *likes* me. And for the first time in a long while, she felt like a girl again, an ordinary girl.

The thought made her happy. Even though the cold was now biting at her toes, her breath was coming in short, quick gasps and her nose was running. She wiped it on her sleeve. Please, God, don't let me get the flu.

She had managed to escape Rosa and the baby. It wasn't hard. Rosa was slow, having to lug Alexi around without Ava to help her; and she mostly stayed in the same place. They usually went home early, as people weren't sympathetic to seeing a baby out late at night. Ava, though, would brave it out. She already had seven euros, and the best time was yet to come! She'd wait for the clubs to start emptying. People coming out, drunk and happy, with cigarettes already in their mouths, patting their pockets in search of a light. And Ava would be there, to save them the trouble: '*Un bricolet, Monsieur/Madam — deux euros, s'il vous plaît!*'

It was going to be a good night. Maybe she'd even make twenty euros! A fortune! Tomorrow she would get takeaway pizza for Papa, and even some beer.

The night wore on. Ava waited around the nightclub area. It was cold, so cold, but she had to hang on. Soon people would start drifting out, and she'd be ready. There were other kids hanging around too, but you could see they were wilting in the cold — shoulders hunched, hopping from foot to foot — they wouldn't last long. She, Ava, would wait it out. She wandered up and down the street, picking up the odd fifty cents just for looking so pathetic and it being Christmas Eve. She looked in the window of her favourite café, the one that looked like a magic cave – soft light around the walls and candles on the table. It was impossible not to imagine what it would be like to sit in there, in the warmth, with a big plate of delicious food. She watched two men at the window table, one drinking coffee, the other eating a sticky, crumbly pastry. Ava's mouth watered. What some people had! If only . . .

She noticed the man nearest the door playing with a phone card, running it through his fingers like a playing card. The bill came. Ava felt as if she was watching a movie. The man put down the card to sign the chit. Then he moved his napkin. The card was hidden. The two men got up, put on their coats. The card was still on the table! Ava thought with a flash of excitement: she could get that card! Ring Gran. After all, it was Christmas Eve. It wouldn't seem strange, even though it was late. And Gran would be *so* happy. She must have been worried, not hearing from them for so long. She knew how the cards worked; they'd used them to call home when they'd first arrived and everything had been good.

Ava was willing the men with all her might, Go, go! Don't remember! And like a miracle, suddenly their coats were on, their scarves around their necks and they were coming out of the door. Without thinking, Ava shot inside like a bullet. In seconds, the card was in her pocket – and no one had seen.

It was getting late. Ava was thinking she couldn't really last much longer. So cold. Not many people were about, not as many – it seemed – as even on a normal night. She felt in her pocket. Hey! She only had one lighter left, anyway. To get rid of that last one, to have sold all of them, would be fantastic news to tell Papa.

Then she saw her luck. Down a little side street, a couple of young men with a girl, swaying about on the pavement. She ran up to them, holding the lighter. '*Un bricolet? Pour vous?*'

One of the boys put his hand in his pocket. This looked promising. The other boy and the girl were leaning against the wall, already smoking.

She didn't see the danger. Until it was too late to move. The boy's fist shot out of his pocket and hit her – thwack! – in the face. She reeled in pain and shock and fell, hard, on the pavement.

The other two laughed. 'Filthy little thieving gypsy brat,' sneered the boy. The girl laughed. Lurching drunkenly away from the wall, she gave a sharp kick to Ava's side. She shoved Ava with her foot, as if she were an animal that she wanted to be sure was dead. Ava moaned.

The other boy looked momentarily anxious. Perhaps they had gone too far?

'She's OK,' said the first boy. 'Leave her. Gypsy brats need to learn a few lessons.'

And then they were off. Staggering down the street, laughing. One of the boys began to sing, '*We wish you a Merry Christmas . . .*'

Maddy sat on the floor with a big pile of presents in front of her. The gorgeous tree was ablaze with light and colour. Mum was lighting candles and Lucy was in the kitchen making some punch – so they can get drunk, Maddy thought scornfully.

They'd hardly said a word to each other all the way home. And then Mum and Lucy had been whispering in the kitchen, about her, Maddy knew. What to do about this terrible turn of events? Maddy, actually standing up for herself for a change.

Then they had come out, all smiles. Pretend it never happened, Maddy guessed that was their plan. Not like Maddy, at all. Blame it on adolescence, and being away from home – she'd never behave like this in England. Well, they were wrong, she was changing, and she knew things. Things they didn't know, and even if they knew they wouldn't care, anyway.

And even with the presents piled invitingly in front of her, Maddy couldn't lift her spirits. She opened each one, saying things like, 'That's nice, thanks,' in a low, flat voice. And even when she opened the big parcel from Mum to find the rucksack she had wanted for ages, longed for in fact, it didn't make a dent in her mood. Mum and Lucy were trying to be all jolly, but it was useless. Some kind of marvellous spell that had been floating around her since they arrived, the special little English-girl spell, was gone for ever.

Ava knew she had to get up. Her side hurt. But she knew it was vital to move. No one was going to help her. If she went to the police, they would make her tell about Papa and arrest them. What was the time? She had no idea.

She pulled herself up and felt a sharp stab of pain. Slowly, she stretched up and got on to her feet. Her face was stinging. She could feel it already swelling up. There was a sharp, bitter taste in her mouth. Blood. She felt with her tongue. A broken tooth.

She felt dizzy with pain and her hands were *so cold*. She put them in her pockets to try to warm them and felt the card. The phone card she had stolen from the table, although it wasn't really stealing, was it? The man had left it behind.

Ava staggered down the little road. Where was she? Her mind was all jumbled, as if her thoughts were frozen and only coming back in little bursts – like a radio going in and out of a tunnel – not making too much sense. She needed to get back to Papa. To the warmth of their stove. But first, yes, she would call Gran, with the card – that's why she had taken it. To phone Gran on Christmas Eve. Wasn't there a phone booth around here somewhere? Her head was spinning. She stumbled to the end of the little street and came out into a wide boulevard. Did she know this place? A few cars, hardly any people. A young couple staggering drunkenly along, their arms around each other. Ava drew back; she knew now what people were, what they could do – suddenly and without warning. She waited in a shop doorway for them to pass. So cold, so cold. She stumbled on   a long way. Surely there would be a phone booth soon. Gran would come, yes. She would come and take her home. And Papa too. It didn't seem like a dream. It was possible. Why not? In her confused mind, Gran was near, only in the next village. All she had to do was phone.

At last, she saw the familiar shape of the glass and metal booths, a whole row of them. It seemed to take ages to reach them. Then she was there, inside. She put the card into the slot – the number, the number? What was the number? It seemed to Ava a matter of life and death that she remembered the number. She knew she had to dial a special code first and when she remembered this, the rest came back to her suddenly, and very clearly.

'Hello? Hello? Who is this?'

Ava didn't know if she could speak. 'Gran.'

'Ava? Ava! Is that you? My God, what time is it for you to be out. What's happened? I've been out of my mind worrying about you. Where are you? Where's Mama and Papa? It's been *months*.'

'I'm OK, Gran. Cold.'

'You're cold, darling? Where's Papa? You *must* tell me. Are you in trouble? I'll come. I'll come. First thing tomorrow, somehow. My God. Just tell me where you are.'

'I don't know.'

'Now, hang on. Stay on the line. Can you find a policeman? Ava, listen to me . . .'

The sound of her grandmother's love was like something warm and real but echoey, like from long ago and far away.

'I'm just ringing to say happy Christmas,' she managed, with a huge effort. 'And I love you. And Papa does too.'

'Ava?'

But the phone went quiet. It fell from the small hand that no longer had the strength to hold it. Her head was light and full of air, as if she might blow away. She slid down the glass to the floor of the booth. She knew she had to sleep, although it was *so* cold. It was her right hand that felt so stiff, like a claw. She put her left hand in her pocket. What's this? A lighter! She had one left. She flicked the wheel and held the flame to her face. She saw, for a moment, her grandmother, smiling.

*

Christmas Eve, very late. Maddy woke suddenly. She had gone to bed early, leaving Mum and Lucy, tipsy and giggly, by themselves. Pathetic. But suddenly now she was wide awake. It must be very late because everything was so quiet, outside only the faint hum of an occasional car. Everyone in this city is sleeping, she thought, except for me. And it felt strange because Maddy usually slept like a dog – unwakeupable, Mum often joked.

The heating was still on, full blast, and her throat felt scratchy and dry. She had an overwhelming desire for a Coke, or fizzy orange. She slid into her new slippers, fluffy penguins with silly wobbly heads (a present from Lucy), and crept into the lounge.

The room was in darkness except for the glow of the tree, and – typical! Mum had left a candle burning on the table by the window. The sort of carelessness which would have earned Maddy a severe telling-off, if it had been her. She fetched her drink from the fridge and sat at the table. Actually, the candle was beautiful. It was like a picture from a storybook, with the tree, and the black sky outside strewn with stars, like a magician's cloak, and the lone silver candle flickering.

Suddenly, Maddy felt a chill – although a moment before the room had seemed as hot as an oven. The feeling fell around her shoulders like a cloak and ran down her arms in a shiver of sadness, like grief, although she wouldn't have been able to name it. She felt a soft but icy draught on her cheek – she turned to see where it could possibly come from. When she turned back, the little flame was out.

*

That Christmas Eve the temperature dropped to the lowest on record. The bitterest cold had descended like an invisible mist, covering the streets of Paris in frost, and claiming all small and helpless things.

This story was inspired by 'The Little Match Girl'. CC